ACROSS THE OTHER POND: U.S. OPPORTUNITIES AND CHALLENGES IN THE ASIA PACIFIC

HEARING

BEFORE THE

SUBCOMMITTEE ON ASIA AND THE PACIFIC

OF THE

COMMITTEE ON FOREIGN AFFAIRS
HOUSE OF REPRESENTATIVES

ONE HUNDRED FOURTEENTH CONGRESS

FIRST SESSION

FEBRUARY 26, 2015

Serial No. 114–8

Printed for the use of the Committee on Foreign Affairs

Available via the World Wide Web: http://www.foreignaffairs.house.gov/ or
http://www.gpo.gov/fdsys/

U.S. GOVERNMENT PUBLISHING OFFICE

93–533PDF   WASHINGTON : 2015

For sale by the Superintendent of Documents, U.S. Government Publishing Office
Internet: bookstore.gpo.gov   Phone: toll free (866) 512–1800; DC area (202) 512–1800
Fax: (202) 512–2104   Mail: Stop IDCC, Washington, DC 20402–0001

CONTENTS

Page

WITNESSES

LETTERS, STATEMENTS, ETC., SUBMITTED FOR THE HEARING

APPENDIX

ACROSS THE OTHER POND: U.S. OPPORTUNITIES AND CHALLENGES IN THE ASIA PACIFIC

THURSDAY, FEBRUARY 26, 2015

House of Representatives,
Subcommittee on Asia and the Pacific,
Committee on Foreign Affairs,
Washington, DC.

The committee met, pursuant to notice, at 10 o'clock a.m., in room 2172 Rayburn House Office Building, Hon. Matt Salmon (chairman of the subcommittee) presiding.

Mr. SALMON. The hearing will come to order. First, I'd like to take this opportunity to welcome everyone to the Asia and Pacific Subcommittee's first hearing of the 114th Congress.

As many of you know, I've spent a significant amount of time living and working in the region, and I'm honored to serve as the chairman of this important subcommittee. I look forward to working with all the committee members to conduct rigorous oversight of our nation's foreign policy and spending decisions in this critical region of the globe.

Since President Obama announced his administration's rebalance to Asia several years ago, the United States has struggled to maintain its priorities to the region. While recognizing the significance of the Asia-Pacific, fiscal austerity at home, and instability and conflict in the Middle East and Eastern Europe have diverted U.S. attention away, and the United States struggles to convince our allies and security partners of our commitment to the region.

Two thousand fifteen will be a pivotal year for U.S. engagement in Asia, presenting numerous economic, political, and security challenges. Today we hope not only to hear about the prospects and obstacles facing the rebalance, but how we could better operationalize our resources to lend greater credence to our objectives in Asia in the medium to long term.

This year we may see the potential passage of the Trans-Pacific Partnership, a 12-member nation trade and investment treaty with Asia-Pacific countries. And there's no doubt that the economic opportunities in the Asia-Pacific are unparalleled. Current negotiating member nations account for 37 percent of total U.S. goods and services trade, so its passage has the prospect to vastly bolster our economic well-being.

Two thousand fifteen will also be a year of continued instability and conflict. In addition to persistent challenges in Asia such as human trafficking, terrorism, human rights violations, catastrophic natural disasters, widespread corruption and ethnic strife, new conflicts and threats will most certainly emerge.

North Korea continues to egregiously violate international norms; from its cyber-attack on Sony Entertainment Pictures late last year to its continued violation of human rights, to its continued pursuit of nuclear weapons capabilities.

Pakistan continues to harbor terrorists and contribute to the instability in the region, and poses a threat to the United States. Various nations' state-sponsored theft of U.S. intellectual property and citizens' personal information presents an enduring, long-term threat to our economic and national security.

This year marks the 70th anniversary of the end of World War II, and Japan's Prime Minister, Shinzo Abe, has proposed revisiting its interpretation of collective self-defense, in light of unprecedented tension between Japan and China. At the same time, the United States and Japan are also revisiting their bilateral defense guidelines. I look forward to hearing what our witnesses think the implications are for the U.S.-Japan alliance.

Later this year, we will also look forward to welcoming India's new leader, Prime Minister Narendra Modi, to the United States. As the world's third largest economy and major democratic power player in Asia, there is immense potential for collaboration and cooperation. Similarly, India also seeks to balance China's growing dominance in the region, and the United States is poised to play a unique role in this space.

We will see whether Burma's reforms since we lifted sanctions have been genuine in its parliamentary elections later this year. And that said, I am concerned with the level of ethnic conflict in Northern Burma between the government and numerous ethnic minority opposition groups, especially the number of displaced refugees the conflict has caused.

Elsewhere in Southeast Asia, political instability has elevated our concern. For example, in Thailand, two military coups over the last 8 years have disrupted our traditionally strong economic and security relationship with that country. Without a clear way forward and no strong domestic governance, Thailand may continue to face significant obstacles.

Finally, China. China continues to gain leverage on the international stage and has challenged international norms of behavior in such areas as diplomacy and cyberspace alike. China has pressured American businesses in unfair, even hostile business environments, while simultaneously partaking in arguably the largest transfer of intellectual property theft in history through means such as cyber espionage. Internally, President Xi Jinping has a brutal anti-corruption campaign to weed out potential opponents while simultaneously clamping down on civilian freedom of expression and access to information.

At the same time, China continues to modernize its military and weapons systems specifically targeted at Taiwan and the United States, and U.S.-allied assets. In the maritime space, China continues to aggravate tensions in the East and South China Seas with its buildup of islands in contested waters and with its aggressive expansionist behavior against its neighbors such as Japan,

Vietnam, and the Philippines under the banner of sovereignty claims. As there is currently no clear solution, I would certainly be interested in hearing from our witnesses today how we can best prevent conflict from escalating and arbitrate these disputes.

China is ostensibly a major factor of the U.S. rebalance, though by no means should our attention to China come at the expense of our other commitments in the region. Our alliances with Japan, South Korea, the Philippines, Australia, and Thailand could help secure cooperation and compliance with international norms.

I really hope that the witnesses will be able to address how the United States can best focus our time and our assets to the rebalance, how we can improve commercial ties, how trade deals like the TPP can help, how we can support democratic governance and transitions, and how we can best support our allies and friends in the region. An improved understanding of U.S. opportunities and challenges in Asia will undoubtedly inform our engagement in the region.

I look forward to hearing from the distinguished witnesses this morning and I now yield to Mr. Sherman, the ranking member of the subcommittee, for his opening remarks.

Mr. SHERMAN. Asia and the Pacific, so many issues, so little time. Glad, Mr. Chairman, you've put together a survey of what our subcommittee will deal with as you begin your chairmanship, and I begin my, what do they call it, ranking membership. And I'm glad to see that so many of us from California and Arizona were able to get through the snow of the East. I don't know if the gentleman from Ohio gets any special accolades for that or not in order to be here today.

This committee's jurisdiction is not only over half the world's population, it is probably over half the world's problems, and half the world's opportunities. A lot of attention is focused on the Muslim world. Our jurisdiction includes Indonesia and Malaysia, the world's two largest—or two of the largest, including Indonesia being the largest democracy in the Muslim world.

Our jurisdiction includes the two nuclear powers that don't have stable governments, North Korea and Pakistan. We are posed to deal with Prime Minister Modi, a new force in India, and the significant trade opportunities that that provides.

And when I mention trade, I should point out that the Trans-Pacific Partnership which is basically a trade deal with Asia is, perhaps, the only legislation this Congress will pass other than, of course, keeping the doors open by passing appropriations bills. Unfortunately, it's legislation we should not pass.

We were told by the International Trade Commission that permanent most favored nation status for China would add $1 billion to our trade deficit. I guess $1 trillion would have been closer. Certainly, several hundred billion dollars per year has been added to— as a result of that decision. And we were told in this room just yesterday by Secretary Kerry that this trade agreement was not a race to the bottom. Well, it's a free trade deal with a country with 30-cent-an-hour wages. how much more bottom do you need to go? How much lower a wage must American workers compete against? And we're told that this trade agreement will confront China, but if you read the Rules of Origin provisions, it will tremendously benefit China.

We can look to our trade agreement with South Korea and see that goods that are 65 percent made in China, sometimes higher, and finished in South Korea get duty-free entry into the United States. Business will eventually take advantage of that, and so China gets all the benefits of a free trade agreement. No, 65 percent of the benefits of a free trade agreement with the United States, and zero percent is what we get of a free trade agreement with China.

It's I think known that I'm a hawk on these trade issues with China. I'm also a dove on the military issues. Most of Washington is on the other side on both of these. The condescension and self-interests of those on the trade issue is, I think, well known. Less well known is just how dedicated the Pentagon is to finding and building us up to confront a worthy adversary. Every time we have confronted a non-uniformed adversary since the Philippine insurrection, it has been an inglorious experience for the Pentagon. Every time we've confronted a worthy uniformed adversary, and there is only one available to us at the present time, it has been a glorious victory and none more glorious than when we defeated the Soviet Union without a major conflagration. So, when I talk to the Pentagon about research, about deployment, about training they say we don't want to prepare for ISIS. There is no glory in Boko Haram; 100 percent of our research dollars are going into how to fight China.

Well, we may get what some wish for; a confrontation with China, but keep in mind these little islands, islets, rocks that are the excuse, even if we win, they're not ours. We build our whole military machine so that Japan, a nation of many islands, gets a couple more. And we're told there's oil there; there isn't, but if there was, it's not ours. So, this buildup to confront China is not in our national interest. It does meet the institutional needs of the Pentagon, and pivot toward Asia seems to be a cover. It is a slogan that conjures up a trade mission to Tokyo, but instead it means spending $½ trillion developing and deploying supersonic fighters that have no purpose other than to hit targets in a well-defended technologically advanced country.

So many issues, so little time. I really haven't mentioned Taiwan, the Philippines, barely mentioned Japan, Burma or Myanmar. We've got a big job to do, and the first step in helping to do that is to yield back to the chair.

Mr. SALMON. There is a little bit of a difference in our opening remarks, and you know what, it's a good thing, it really is. I have nothing but respect for the ranking member. And while we're probably going to come to some different conclusions, I have nothing but respect for the positions that you've taken. I think they've always been principled, and I believe that unlike a lot of politicians here in Washington, DC, you actually believe what you say, and I have nothing but respect for that.

Mr. SHERMAN. Can I use that in my next campaign?

Mr. SALMON. I'm not sure it will help you coming from me.

If other members would like to make an opening statement, go ahead, absolutely.

Mr. CHABOT. I'll be brief. I just wanted to, first of all, congratulate you on your chairmanship, your first hearing, and wish you the best. Having had the honor to chair this subcommittee in the last Congress, I know that you're more than up to the job. Speaking Chinese is something that I never accomplished; I really never accomplished speaking in any other language other than English, but you've mastered it. And, I think you're perfectly positioned to chair this subcommittee. I know you're going to do it well.

I also know that Mr. Sherman will do a great job, even though we may disagree on an issue here or there. He is principled, and one of the smartest guys in Congress. He'll let you know that once in a while. No, I won't say that, no. Just by your actions you'll let us know, not by informing us. I know having traveled with Mr. Sherman to Asia in the last Congress, I think over time I would consider him not just a colleague, but a friend. And periodically, we find an issue to agree on, and that's a good thing.

I also want to congratulate and commend Mr. Bera for filling in for Eni Faleomavaega in the last Congress as ranking member. Eni, as we all know, had some serious health issues that he was dealing with much of that Congress, and Ami did a great job. At the same time, he had a barn-burner of a race back home, which I'm familiar since I've had a number of those over the years. My district has changed, and I hopefully won't have that any time in the near future, but experience that time and again. When you are in one of those races, it can be challenging to really put in the time and effort up here, and I always try to do that. I know Mr. Bera did, as well, so I want to commend him for that.

I actually having another hearing going on, so I'm going to be going between two places. I'm the new chairman of the Small Business Committee, the first time I've chaired a full committee, so that's something that I'm going to be devoting a lot of attention. But Foreign Affairs is near and dear to my heart, having served on this committee for 19 years now; the full committee, and chaired the Middle East Subcommittee. That said, the Asia-Pacific region is critically important, and when you consider the amount of trade that goes through that area, and the world's oil shipments—two-thirds of the oil shipments—it's a critical part of the world.

The so-called ''rebalancing'' or ''pivot,'' I think in concept, at least, may be a good one. I think there's some question about the follow-up, particularly when one considers the growing, for lack of a better term, chaos in the Middle East; whether it's Yemen, which was touted as kind of a success story and recently we saw the government fall to an Iranian-backed Hoothi group; to Libya, where we saw 21 Christians literally beheaded on the beach there recently. There's a whole range of things we can talk about in the Middle East, so I understand why the rebalance certainly may not be as it was originally envisioned—we're not necessarily seeing that right now.

Those are the kind of questions I'd ask, but I have to go to another committee. What can we expect from that rebalance when you consider what's actually going on in the Middle East? It looks like not only are we going to be exiting that region to some degree, I think we're going to be going back in, in considerable form in the very near future.

So, anyway, thank you and congratulations on your chairmanship, and I yield back my time, Mr. Salmon.

Mr. SALMON. Thank you, very much. Mr. Bera, would you like to
make an opening statement?

Mr. BERA. Sure, and I'll keep mine short. I'm looking forward to
a great session of Congress with you, Mr. Chairman, and the new
ranking member. I'm also looking forward to the testimony of the
witnesses.

Obviously, I have a keen interest in the U.S.-South Asia, U.S.-
India relationship. Also, very interested in getting an update on,
you know, some of the tensions in the South China Sea, as well as
it does seem like things in the East China Sea have settled down
a little bit, but again these unilateral moves that China has made,
and getting that update.

Again, I think we're going to have a great session of Congress.
I think there is huge opportunity both geopolitically and economically in a strong U.S.-Asia relationship. And, obviously, just having
returned from India, I think there is huge opportunity and promise
in the U.S.-India relationship, both strategically and economically.
So, look forward to the testimony.

Mr. SALMON. Thank you. Mr. Lowenthal, yes.

Mr. LOWENTHAL. Thank you, Mr. Chairman, ranking members,
and all the witnesses. It's a real pleasure to join this subcommittee.

I, like many of my colleagues, think that we have tremendous—
we're at a pivotal point in U.S. foreign policy in Asia. I think there
are lots of opportunities, but there are also great challenges. You
know, as we continue to see greater involvement and engagement,
especially through the TPP, that raises certain issues for me.

I represent the Port of Long Beach and know how critical the engagement of all these countries are at an economic level. And while
we grapple with issues of environment and the TPP, labor, currency manipulation, and state-owned enterprises, for example, we
also now have unprecedented leverage in these negotiations to promote universal values of human rights.

I believe if you want to gain favorable trading status with the
United States and your neighbors, you must at least adhere to a
minimal standard of respecting the basic rights of your own citizens. So for me in my district, and what I'm concerned about is,
for example, Vietnam. It's failed time and time again to meet anything close to a minimal standard. This one party authoritarian
government represses, sometimes violently, anyone who speaks out
against the regime. The government jails bloggers, labor activists,
and religious leaders seemingly on a whim.

You know, while Vietnam has been increasingly pressured by the
international community to improve its human rights record in recent years, it seems like every step forward is also accompanied by
two steps backward.

I look forward to hearing the witnesses, not only in terms of economic issues, and security issues, but really how we can advocate
for values that are not just important to us as Americans, but really are universal values. And I look forward to really the discussion
that takes place on this committee.

Mr. SALMON. Thank you. Representative Meng.

Ms. MENG. Thank you, Chairman Salmon, and Ranking Member Sherman for welcoming me. I'm very honored to join the Subcommittee on Asia and the Pacific this term.

Our hearing today is aptly named. This is an important time for many Asian countries that are rising in economic strength, and looking to increase their power in the region, and globally. The strength of our relationships with these countries will be a defining characteristic of the next century.

I look forward to working with my colleagues as we navigate these relationships, and work with our allies in the region.

Mr. SALMON. Thank you very much. We're pleased to have such an excellent panel join us today to share their expertise on this very important region of the world.

First, Dr. Karl Jackson serves as the Director of the Asian Studies Program at Johns Hopkins School of Advanced International Studies, where he founded the Southeast Asian Studies Program. Before he joined Johns Hopkins University, Dr. Jackson served as the Vice President's National Security Advisor and as Special Assistant to the President.

Dr. Van Jackson is currently a visiting Fellow at the Center for a New American Security. Prior to joining CNAS, Dr. Jackson served with distinction in the Office of the Secretary of Defense. Dr. Jackson also lectures at a number of highly regarded academic institutions, including Georgetown University and Catholic University of America.

Mr. Matthew Goodman joins us from the Center for Strategic and International Studies, where he's a Senior Advisor for Asian Economics. Mr. Goodman previously served in numerous roles in the administration, including the Departments of State and Treasury, as well as the White House.

Mr. Abraham Denmark is the Senior Vice President for Political and Security Affairs at the National Bureau of Asian Research. Before his time at NBR, Mr. Denmark was a professional in both the private sector and the government, and worked in the Office of the Secretary of Defense.

Mr. Patrick Mulloy was most recently a five-term Commissioner of the Bipartisan U.S.-China Security and Economic Review Commission. Mr. Mulloy is a trade lawyer and former Assistant Secretary in the Department of Commerce's International Trade Administration.

And without objection, the witnesses fully prepared statements will be made part of the record, and members will have 5 calendar days to submit statements, questions, and extraneous materials for the record.

Let me just briefly explain the lighting system. I'm sure you're all familiar with it. You each are given 5 minutes for your prepared statements. After 4 minutes, you'll see an amber light, just to let you know that it's coming close. When the light hits red, it's time to conclude. I've not been a real stickler if you go a few seconds over because I really want to hear what you have to say. The same thing for members' questions. We don't want them to go on forever, but I really do have a light gavel. If you've got questions you want answered, that's why we're here, so if you go a few seconds over, don't worry. Let's just get as much as we can.

8

So with that, we're going to start with you, Dr. Jackson, and we'll work our way over.

STATEMENT OF KARL D. JACKSON, PH.D., C.V. STARR DISTINGUISHED PROFESSOR OF SOUTHEAST ASIA STUDIES, DIRECTOR OF THE ASIAN STUDIES PROGRAM, JOHNS HOPKINS SCHOOL OF ADVANCED INTERNATIONAL STUDIES

Mr. KARL JACKSON. Thank you very much, Mr. Chairman, and other distinguished members of the committee. I used to testify as a government witness; now I'm a free man, but that was a long time ago in the age of Steve Solarz and Jim Leach. But, in any case, it's good to be back in front of the committee, and I'm not going to read my statement. I'd like to just make a few points so that we can get on to my younger brother, Dr. Van Jackson.

The first point I'd like to make is, Asia has in our lifetimes been a remarkably successful place. It's been far more successful than we ever thought, at least I ever thought as a young adult. There's been a larger increase in prosperity in a shorter amount of time than mankind has ever witnessed.

This is an amazing turn of events, but with that turn of events comes greater complexity because China and India are going to be much, much more powerful in the next 25 years than we ever anticipated really 30 to 40 years ago. The so called uni-polar moment of the United States in Asia, in my opinion, has passed, and we will be facing a multi-polar balance of power in Asia, and we have to figure out how to deal with it so that we preserve our own interests, but also avoid conflict.

Now, I'd say the last time the world faced the problem of integrating two new big rising powers we failed miserably. We have two World Wars, as a result, and the name of the game for us in the 21st century, and the assignment for the next generation, is to avoid repeating the follies of the 20th century.

I would contend that we have to bring to the head table of international relations both India and China, and to combine them in a quadri-partite conflict prevention mechanism that deals only with security, not with trade, not with human rights, not with many other incredibly important issues, but I contend that the biggest problem we face in Asia is to prevent these disputes over worthless rocks escalating into warfare which would destroy both the peace and prosperity of the Pacific.

Several members mentioned the rebalance. I think it's very important to make sure that the rebalance is not under-resourced on the military side. I think it's incredibly important to make sure that TPP and the trade side receive the prominence that they deserve. And I think it's enormously important that the rebalance be conceptualized as running all the way from India around the Horn to Korea, and all the way down under; otherwise, it becomes just a synonym for a China containment strategy which, in my opinion, if that is approached unilaterally with just the United States, or just the United States and Japan, it won't work.

So, I would contend that U.S. policy over the next 5 years should give just as much attention to the U.S.-India relationship as it gives to the U.S.-China relationship, as it gives to the U.S.-Japan relationship. Why? We need to have four powers together potentially in the same room at a very high level to insure that we will not allow some of the things that Mr. Sherman mentioned to escalate into warfare. Thank you. I yield to my older brother.

[The prepared statement of Mr. Karl Jackson follows:]

Feb 24

Testimony of Karl D. Jackson

C.V. Starr Distinguished Professor of Southeast Asian Studies

School of Advanced International Studies

Johns Hopkins University

Before the

House Committee on Foreign Affairs

Sub Committee on Asia and the Pacific

February 26, 2015

Asia, overall, is a major long-term success story for US foreign policy. This is not the Ukraine, Libya, Syria, Iraq, or Afghanistan. No wars are taking place in Asia. Rapid economic growth began in Asia during the 1970s and Asia has witnessed the greatest increase in wealth, for the largest number of people, in the shortest time, in the history of mankind. Terrorism has largely been contained. Even though there has been some regression, more Asians live in democracies than we would have thought possible a few decades ago. What we need now is a strategy for dealing with the more complex world generated by success in Asia.

Because Asia has been on a positive trajectory for the last thirty-five years the natural temptation is to forget about it, focusing on today's hot spots while ignoring the coming challenges that a rising Asia will pose for U.S. policy. A steady American devotion of moderate military, economic, and diplomatic resources to Asia now may allow us to avoid major tensions and even conflict in the future. Steady attention to all of Asia now, from India around to Korea and all the way down under to Australia and New Zealand, will give us a better chance of integrating two rising, major powers (China and India) into a peaceful and prosperous structure similar to the one we have maintained since the end of World War II.

The last time the world faced the task of integrating two major powers into the international system, statecraft failed miserably. Two world wars resulted from a failure to either include or deter Germany and Imperial Japan when they became more powerful at the dawn of the 20th century. China and India are emerging as part of a multi-polar Asian balance of power. The job of the next generation of soldiers, diplomats, legislators, business leaders, and policy intellectuals is to ensure that 21st century history will not repeat the follies of the 20th century. The mantle of leadership that fell on the United States on the 7th of December 1941 cannot now be abandoned without disastrous consequences. The United States, along with its allies, must convince China and India that they each have more to gain through collective moderation than through nationalist revisionism. This must involve both diplomacy and deterrence, both carrots and sticks, and it can only work if there is steady leadership from Washington that will resist the temptation of leaving Asia's problems to another day and thereby allowing them to fester until they become insolvable.

The Challenges

All emerging power-holders bring to the international system a sense of entitlement and a desire to change things rapidly in their favor. They have never been so powerful before, and like all newcomers they dream that the future belongs to them. From time to time, political challenges at home may prompt these emerging powers to adopt uncompromising nationalistic stances abroad, especially in disputes where the physical stakes are small but are defined in the emotional terms of national identity. While rising powers demand more space, established powers are reluctant to yield appropriate portions of power and prestige to the newcomers. Just when the international system most needs a burst of creativity, inertia remains the predictable norm.

What we are witnessing in Asia is the rise of two new powers, China and India. Inevitably they will increase their defense budgets very substantially, and this will certainly compel the established powers such as Japan, Korea, the Southeast Asian countries, and the United States to increase their deployments in response. The question is how to slow the upward spiral and still deter the emerging power-holders from taking actions over questions of identity that may drag the entire system into conflict? Can we not find a new way of increasing the stature of the emerging powers in ways that will ensure peace rather than threaten it?

A Strategy

A new paradigm is necessary to channel the inevitable tensions that will be generated by much larger and more powerful air and naval forces. What I am suggesting is creating of an Asia Pacific Council consisting exclusively of the Big Four (China, India, Japan, and the U.S.). Since the late 1980s, Asia has witnessed the creation of one multi-lateral organization after another: APEC, ARF, EAS to cite just a few. Almost all of these concern themselves primarily with trade and economic integration while avoiding the critical questions that actually bedevil the international system in Asia - questions of territory and national identity. Each existing organization contains too many actors. Rather than creating another talk shop, the purpose of an Asia Pacific Council is to have a powerful group that can be convened informally whenever there is a security crisis. Only a small group can constrain a crisis, by removing any ambiguities about where the major powers stand and by putting major leaders in the same room. Rather than seeking paper resolutions, the Asia-Pacific Council would be an emergency response mechanism for preventing the escalation of local conflict situations and for the maintaining constant contact at the foreign minister level. An Asia Pacific Council may be necessary to calm the roiling waters by involving the major naval powers of Asia and the Pacific in an elevated process of crisis prevention through rapid communication and interaction whenever a crisis is brewing in the South China Sea, the East China Sea, or elsewhere. Creating the diplomatic equivalent of a quadripartite hot line would restrain powers from undertaking unilateral actions because of the inevitability of a concerted challenge to unilateral measures by the other members of the Big Four. The purpose of an Asia Pacific Council would be to recognize the rising status of China and India and to reward them with an involvement in 21st century rule making that would be both real and exclusive. Rather than just calling for rules-based conflict avoidance, the United States should take the lead in sitting down with the leading air and naval powers of the Asia-Pacific to devise rules for precluding conflict and for streamlining arbitration procedures.

In the meantime, the U.S., as the primary established power, must maintain a meaningful forward military presence and continue to engage in steady diplomatic efforts to preserve and promote a stable security framework as well as a system of international trade in which both Asians and Americans have prospered. Again the problem will be to convince the emerging powers that their long-term benefits will be maximized by actively participating in a modified international architecture that recognizes their emerging status while maintaining peace and prosperity throughout Asia and the Pacific.

The Rebalance to Asia must be multi-faceted and involve all of Asia rather than just a concern for China. Sending Marines to Darwin, rotating air and naval assets through the Philippines and home porting naval vessels in Singapore only makes sense if there is an equal emphasis on creating a new economic infrastructure for Asia and the Pacific. A Rebalance to Asia that does not have new military and economic resources will be dismissed as public relations puffery rather than a strategy. Likewise a Rebalance to Asia that does not involve India will be dismissed as just a new name for containing China.

U.S.

Not only must the United States remain the preeminent naval and air power in Asia but it must be perceived to be so. An inevitable by-product of the growth of both China and India will be a narrative about "America in decline." This story is an old one. "Soviet superiority" now seems an odd phrase. Likewise, the statement, "The Cold War is over and Japan won," is more amusing than accurate. Nonetheless we are looking toward a multi-polar balance of power in Asia. This is why the US should take a leading role actively bringing the new powers to the high table of international politics by taking an active role in designing new trade and security structures. Continuing to be the major force in international affairs is not compatible with the currently envisioned force cuts. Regardless of what we say, Asian nations, be they friend or foe, will judge U.S. intentions by its capabilities and accept or reject U.S. leadership as a consequence. If we make "we can't do everything, everywhere" our public mantra, our intentions will be tested everywhere to determine the exact limits of what we mean.

Japan

Japan is the most important ally of the United States in Asia. Hence the United States retains a critical interest in Japan's economy and national security policies. The current prime minister of Japan is unusual in that he will be prime minister for at least four years rather than just for a year like his immediate predecessors. Prime Minister Abe's first priority is to reform the Japanese economy by transferring the high productivity of the export manufacturing sector into the service and agricultural sectors. Joining the U.S. in the Trans Pacific Partnership can provide a motive for accomplishing domestic economic reforms that have been long overdue in Japan. Prime Minister Abe's desire to remove some of the restrictions that the U.S. imposed on Japan during the constitution writing process nearly seventy years ago is understandable but political realities within his own coalition will naturally limit this process. Japan's military posture has changed and its defense budget is rising. The changes taking place in Japan are profoundly unsettling to China and Korea but Japan perceives its altered stance as having been forced upon it by the unsettling behaviors of China. This is a classic security dilemma that can only be cured by a combination of deterrence and increased diplomatic activity. Silence is the worst option.

China

China has risen, and fulfilling Napoleon Bonaparte's prophecy, it is shaking the world. It is already a massive economic power and well on its way to becoming a military power capable of projecting its influence well beyond its coastal areas. Like all rising powers it dreams have yet to be fully tempered by the cold water of reality. In the future China's growth will slow because growth always slows with economic maturation. In addition China will need to adapt to a future in which the United States will become more active in constraining China's assertiveness toward traditional U.S. friends and allies. The easy part of China's rise is now over and the question is whether the next, more economically difficult phases, will be managed with the astuteness of a Deng or the petulance of a Mao? General Secretary Xi Jinping seems to fall somewhere in between. Xi has taken full control of the party and the military and has set forth an anti-corruption campaign aimed at restoring the moral legitimacy of the Communist Party while conveniently humbling his political opponents. In foreign policy he has adopted a distinctively more assertive policy toward Japan, the Philippines, and Vietnam. His China dream is a revisionist one, and the fundamental questions remain: how much risk he feels he must take to maintain his domestic support base and how much risk to the international system his strategy will entail?

U.S. clarity can ensure that China will understand: 1) that the U.S. does not accept Chinese sovereignty over the South China Sea; 2) that the U.S. sides with Japan on the relationship of the U.S.-Japan Security Arrangement to the Senkaku/Diaoyu controversy; 3) that if provoked the U.S. will match Chinese military assertiveness by increasing its military presence in Australia, the Philippines, and Singapore, as well as providing increased diplomatic support for Vietnam; 4) that any use of force regarding Taiwan continues to be unacceptable and that any moves in this direction will increase rather than decrease arms sales to Taiwan. Reiteration of these "red lines" through normal diplomatic channels remains important, even when reiteration is met with blunt rejection. Verbal assertion of freedom of navigation remains insufficient. U.S. naval and air presence in the South China Sea and the East China Sea must be maintained or increased. Chinese policy makers can determine by their own actions whether they will have a smooth or a rough relationship with the U.S. but the U.S. must remain ready to respond accordingly. Rather than trying single-handedly to contain China, we need to build an Asia wide strategy to convince China (under a variety of leaders) that it is better to play in a peaceful and cooperative sandbox than it is to create incidents and to practice raw mercantilism toward the outside world.

India

As Henry Kissinger recently remarked, China, Japan, and India are each currently led by unusually strong and assertive leaders. For decades India remained off the U.S. policy radar screen during the Cold War, but since the mid-1990s India and the United States have moved, slowly but steadily closer to one another. A strong India, working in tandem with the United States, could be a powerful source of moderation, especially with regard to the maritime disputes plaguing East and Southeast Asia. India's greatest strength lies in its democratic system which contains a set of stable procedures for replacing parties and leaders. Although Indian democracy is messy, it is inherently stable. Policies do not move in autocratically straight lines but the system of government contains the safety valves that are necessary for Indian society to continue to move forward toward rapid economic development. Defense expenditures always rise with rapid economic growth, and India will be no exception. U.S. policy should seek to influence rather than to direct India. India, as a rising power, will have its own dreams. By bringing India to the high table of international politics, alongside China, Japan, and the U.S., India's prestige and influence will be increased as it joins the Big Four Asia-Pacific naval and air powers. To make this relationship work the United States must put as much effort into U.S.-India relations as it does currently into U.S.-China and U.S.-Japan relations. Rather than resist the expiration of the brief uni-polar world of the immediate post-Cold War era, the United States must learn to play nimbly in a four-sided diplomatic game to ensure peace and stability in a new and more prosperous and powerful Asia.

Mr. SALMON. Thank you. Dr. Jackson.

STATEMENT OF VAN JACKSON, PH.D., VISITING FELLOW, CENTER FOR A NEW AMERICAN SECURITY

Mr. VAN JACKSON. Thank you. Mr. Chairman, Ranking Member Sherman, distinguished members of the subcommittee, let me just say that I'm a great fan of both California and Arizona. And thank you for the opportunity to come address this topic today.

U.S.-Asia policy should not be autopilot. Right? It merits regular critical scrutiny most intensely at times when the regional landscape is changing, and I would offer that that time is today. If I have a singular assertion it's that over the next 2 years, keeping Asia stable should be the overwhelming priority for U.S. policy in Asia.

The Trans-Pacific Partnership, human rights, fostering democratic political transitions in authoritarian regimes, all of this matters, but none of it's possible in a region riven with conflict, so it may sound banal to prioritize keeping Asia stable, but it means adapting to what I would describe as greater structural risks facing the region.

The chairman mentioned some of these. China is demonstrating an increased willingness to challenge the international status quo. At the same time, we have Japan seeking to expand its security role in the region after half a century of formalized pacifism in international affairs. Militaries across the Asia-Pacific are undertaking robust arms buildups, military modernization programs, increasing the latent capacity for rapid destruction in the event of conflict. And North Korea is expanding and improving its nuclear and ballistic missile programs completely unchecked, even as it finds novel ways to coerce, to probe the resolve of the United States and its South Korean ally.

All of these developments are taking place against a backdrop of region-wide mistrust, uncertainty about the future, and long-standing unresolved territorial disputes. Taken together, these circumstances constrain the ability for even astute statesmen to navigate Asia peacefully.

I would submit that keeping Asia stable amid these evolving circumstances require two things from the U.S. First, to be seen as a sure thing, as a reliable ally and partner. To the extent uncertainty drives regional security trends in a problematic or undesirable direction, certainty about the U.S. can help be an antidote for that. And then second, I think we need to do what we can to encourage the militarization of the region in a defensive direction. And I think this can be achieved by working with regional allies and partners to develop military capabilities and operational concepts that improves overall situational awareness, counter the ability of others to project power, and strengthen territorial integrity of sovereign borders.

In short, I think it would benefit the region and the United States to empower the region's smaller and middle powers to better defend themselves; particularly, as dominant military technologies evolve and spread. Despite growing economic interdependence among Asian states, the region remains a potential powder keg.

China is still a lingering concern for most, but so are the long-term intentions of neighbors among middle powers, to say nothing of the risks that North Korea may pose as it develops a survivable nuclear force. The United States rightly seeks a peaceful, liberal order in Asia, and I would suggest that the minimal necessary condition for that to obtain is stability, which is facing greater structural risk. So, thank you again, and I look forward to answering your questions.

[The prepared statement of Mr. Van Jackson follows:]

Testimony before the House Committee on Foreign Affairs
Subcommittee on Asia and the Pacific
Prepared Statement of Dr. Van Jackson
Visiting Fellow, Center for a New American Security
February 26, 2015

Mr. Chairman and members of the subcommittee, thank you very much for granting me the opportunity to testify today. I am honored to take part in this session.[1]

The subject of this hearing, regional opportunities and constraints, is precisely how a discussion on Asia should be framed because as regional trends and country-specific circumstances change, so too do the options available for U.S. policy.

U.S. security contributions and its shaping influence in regional affairs have prevented Asia from reviving the "might makes right" pattern of conflict and insecurity that characterized much of Asia's pre-Cold War history. For more than a generation, the U.S. military presence in Asia, along with its network of alliances and partnerships, has helped maintain stability and a semblance of order. Asia is economically vibrant and increasingly modern because a relatively stable security climate has endured.

Yet, as ever, numerous territorial disputes, unresolved historical legacies, and competing strands of nationalism contribute to several well-known flashpoints in Asia: islands in the East China Sea between China and Japan; parts of the Yellow Sea between North and South Korea; disputed island territory between Japan and South Korea; and a lattice of overlapping South China Sea claimants, both within the Association of Southeast Asian Nations (ASEAN) and between ASEAN nations and China. It may be tempting to conclude from the absence of war in Asia for the past several decades that concerns about Asia's many flashpoints are overblown; competent statesmen can prevent simmering tensions from boiling over into conflict. And at any rate, the massive growth of economic ties among Asian states makes violent conflict of any type wholly irrational.

But Asia's surface-level calm and incentives for peace belie a disturbing undercurrent. The contemporary Asian security environment is undergoing several subtle but detectable shifts that not only introduce greater risks to the U.S. position in Asia, but also to the prospect of continued peace in the region. I wish to bring to your attention three such trends. First, states that challenge the status quo are increasingly doing so in ways that are deniable, by pursuing types of coercion that make attribution difficult, or that blur the distinction between aggressor and defender. Second, military buildups, weapons modernization programs, and select forms of arms racing are now

---

[1] Parts of this written testimony draw from Van Jackson, *Reshaping the Rebalance: How the 114th Congress Can Advance U.S. Asia Strategy* (Seattle: National Bureau of Asian Research, 2015); Van Jackson, "The Rise and Persistence of Strategic Hedging across Asia: A System-Level Analysis," in *Strategic Asia 2014-15: U.S. Alliances and Partnerships at the Center of Global Power*, edited by Ashley Tellis, Abraham Denmark, and Greg Chaffin (Seattle: National Bureau of Asian Research, 2014).

www.cnas.org

region-wide phenomena. Third, North Korea's nuclear program is not simply growing unchecked; it is on track to eventually securing an assured retaliatory nuclear strike capability.

These trends overlay Asia's existing tensions, making the region's longstanding security challenges more combustible than in the past. Given these changes, the U.S. military presence and security commitments in Asia are more important than ever. At the same time, U.S. policy in Asia cannot remain stagnant; it must adapt to, and to the extent possible capitalize on, the ways the region is changing to ensure continued stability. Keeping Asia stable amid change remains the core regional challenge for the next two years.

The Emergence of "Gray Zone" Coercion

When scholars and policymakers think of coercion between states, they typically picture militaries sending unambiguous signals of resolve, employing military force or the threat of force to achieve political aims.[2] In recent years, however, states seeking to forcefully pursue political goals have resorted to an approach sometimes described as "gray zone" coercion because it defies obvious classification as either a peacetime or wartime action.[3]

In the East and South China Seas, China has engaged in a pattern of assertiveness over territorial claims without directly employing People's Liberation Army naval forces, instead relying on non-traditional actors and non-traditional means—fishing vessels, the Coast Guard, water cannons, construction crews that build artificial islands in disputed areas, intrusive but unarmed reconnaissance drones, and "sonic devices" that induce nausea in their targets.[4] But gray zone coercion is not unique to China. North Korea has employed this type of unconventional coercion as well, ranging from the 2010 sinking of the South Korean ship *CHEONAN*[5]—which North Korea conducted in a way that allowed it to deny responsibility—to the multiple intrusions of North Korean drones into South Korean airspace in 2013 and 2014,[6] as well as the cyber coercion against Sony Studios by a proxy hacker group late last year.[7] All of these events share in common the use of coercion to further a political agenda, but with either non-traditional actors (hacker groups and non-military or paramilitary entities) or non-traditional means (unlabeled drones, cyberattacks, and clandestine military attacks).

---

[2] This is the classical conception of rational coercion. See, for example, Thomas Schelling, *Arms and Influence* (New Haven: Yale University Press, 1966).

[3] See, for example, Patrick Cronin, *The Challenge of Responding to Maritime Coercion* (Washington, DC: CNAS, 2014).

[4] Amy Chang, Ben FitzGerald, and Van Jackson, *Shades of Gray: Technology, Stability, and Strategic Competition in Maritime Asia* (Washington, DC: CNAS, 2015).

[5] "North Korean Torpedo Sank South's Navy Ship," *BBC*, May 20, 2010.

[6] Van Jackson, "Kim Jong Un's Tin Can Air Force," *Foreign Policy*, November 1, 2014.

[7] Mark Seal, "An Exclusive Look Inside Sony's Hacking Saga," *Vanity Fair*, March 2015, http://www.vanityfair.com/hollywood/2015/02/sony-hacking-seth-rogen-evan-goldberg.

The distinct danger in gray zone coercion is that it shifts the initiative to escalate a crisis—and potentially the ability to control it—from the aggressor to the defender by altogether blurring the distinction between them. This can benefit the aggressor in multiple ways.

First, it can induce decision-making paralysis that prevents the victim of coercion from retaliating. This is arguably what occurred with China's drone intrusion into contested territory with Japan, the latter being uncertain how to interpret the drone intrusion because it was aggressive, but also unarmed. North Korea's 2010 sinking of the *CHEONAN* had this effect as well, raising doubts within South Korea about whether North Korea even committed the attack simply because North Korea denied it. In both cases, the coercing state prevented retaliation by sewing doubts about the fact of aggression and who was responsible.

Second, aggressive states might also be motivated to undertake gray zone coercion because it allows them to fracture international consensus and claim moral high ground in the event the defender chooses to retaliate. If, for example, Southeast Asian states react to Chinese fishing vessels in the contested Spratly Islands with traditional military forces, they—not the Chinese—might be accused of escalating the conflict. If China then retaliates or escalates in kind, it can rally domestic opinion by claiming it is the victim of external aggression.

Increasingly, it appears that when Asian states choose to push back against the status quo, they resort more readily to gray zone coercion than traditional gunboat diplomacy or straightforward military attacks. Despite eschewing outright military violence initially, gray zone coercion is now occurring with greater frequency than traditional coercion and represents a manipulation of risk that makes miscalculations and inadvertent escalation more likely than in the past.

Asia's Military Buildup

Across Asia, militaries large and small are undergoing intense modernization programs that improve the capacity of each to conduct violent military campaigns. China's military spending and capability development are well documented,[8] but military modernization is a region-wide trend, as evidenced by qualitative improvements in payload capacity, range, technological complexity, doctrine, and overall asymmetry relative to the militaries of potential competitors.

Taiwan is undergoing a comprehensive military modernization program ranging from upgraded point missile defense to procuring new minesweepers, attack helicopters, and naval surface vessels.[9] Similarly, the Philippines has 24 modernization projects underway, including new multipurpose attack vessels, upgraded fighter aircraft, and improved maritime surveillance capabilities.[10] The Indonesian military is allocating roughly one-third of its entire defense budget

---

[8] For an official assessment of China's military modernization, see Office of the Secretary of Defense, *Annual Report to Congress: Military and Security Developments Involving the People's Republic of China 2013* (Washington, DC: 2013).

[9] "Taiwan's Force Modernization: The American Side," *Defense Industry Daily*, June 4, 2014.

[10] Richard Jacobson, "Modernizing the Philippine Military," *The Diplomat*, August 22, 2013.

for the fiscal period 2010-14 to wholesale modernization across all warfighting domains.[11] Australia and Singapore are both moving in the direction of advanced fighter aircraft procurement with their respective decisions to pursue the F-35. Vietnam has increased investments in maritime patrol craft and begun acquiring fast attack submarines from Russia.[12] Myanmar, which has focused most of its military effort internally in recent decades, is looking to produce the Sino-Pakistani JF-17, a multirole fighter aircraft that is a better fit for fighting foreign militaries than domestic rebellions.[13] And Japan, despite being the only nation with a constitution that foreswears war has increased its role in Asian security and "collective defense," alongside maintaining its regional superiority in ballistic missile defense, upgrading its fighter aircraft to the F-35, increasing investments in antisubmarine warfare, and beginning amphibious landing exercises with the United States.[14]

Left unaddressed, this trend poses greater risks to regional stability over time because of other tensions and mistrust that linger in the background. The region's militarization inherently creates a greater latent capacity for violence regardless of what the dispute may be. If this trend endures, so too does the risk of a security dilemma generating undesirable military competition. Even if an Asian state supports the status quo and is uninterested in conquering others, there is still a high prospect that seeing one's neighbors build and field advanced militaries will generate feelings of insecurity that compel it to do the same.[15] These security dilemma dynamics can increase pressure for war even if nobody seeks conflict.

North Korea's Improving Nuclear Capabilities
For the past generation, the United States has pursued two overarching goals relating to North Korea: (1) preventing North Korea from becoming a nuclear state and (2) preventing the renewed outbreak of war on the Korean Peninsula. The United States has acutely and visibly failed at the first goal: North Korea is not only now a de facto nuclear state, but the size of its arsenal is unknown, and Pyongyang is progressing toward its own version of a secure retaliatory nuclear strike capability.[16] The second goal is increasingly at risk of failure because the first goal has failed. If it does not already, North Korea may soon believe it has a free hand to engage in various forms of coercive violence and military adventurism precisely because it thinks it has a nuclear deterrent

---

[11] Tiarma Siboro, "Indonesia, U.S. Deepen Defense Ties amid Exercises and Arms Deals," *Defense News*, September 30, 2013.

[12] Daniel Bodirsky, "Vietnam's Naval Modernization Threatens to Destabilize Region," *Global Risk Insights*, April 1, 2014.

[13] Zackary Keck, "Burma to Purchase Chinese-Pakistani JF-17 Fighter Jets," *The Diplomat*, June 25, 2014.

[14] Greg Waldron, "In Focus: China Crisis Adds Urgency to Japanese Air Force Modernisation," *Flight International*, October 8, 2012; James Hardy, "Japan's Navy: Sailing Towards the Future," *The Diplomat*, January 21, 2013.

[15] Robert Jervis, *Perception and Misperception in International Politics* (Princeton: Princeton University Press, 1976).

[16] In the nuclear deterrence literature, a secure retaliatory strike capability implies that a nuclear power could not be fully disarmed by a first strike, which enhances the deterrent effect of a nuclear arsenal because a first strike would invite nuclear retaliation. When two nuclear powers each have such a capability, the condition of mutually assured destruction is thought to obtain, rendering the prospect of nuclear war—in theory—extremely low.

against major war.[17] In 2010, North Korea aimed these acts of coercive violence directly at South Korea, triggering multiple military crises in which U.S. and South Korean preferences for retaliation and conflict escalation vastly diverged.[18] For decades, U.S. policymakers have grudgingly accepted small-scale North Korean violence as an alternative preferable to risking a larger conflagration.[19] But as North Korea moves closer to a retaliatory nuclear strike capability, it also moves closer to being able to set the terms of conflict with South Korea. If South Korea deems the prospect of continuous small wars or repeated acts of coercion unacceptable—as it did in 2010—the United States will lose the ability to prevent war on the Korean Peninsula.

North Korea's cyber capability has received much attention after the country proved in 2014 that it could attack U.S.-based corporations, but this capability is only lethal in conjunction with other weapons systems. More disconcerting is North Korea's drone fleet, which has demonstrated the ability to repeatedly penetrate South Korean airspace undetected and, with modest payload improvements, could be configured as weapons delivery systems.[20] Still more dangerous are developments in North Korea's ballistic missile program. It has been reported that North Korea's short-range Rodong ballistic missiles, once thought primarily useful for striking bases in Japan because of their range, have now been tested at new launch angles that allow it to fire against South Korean targets as well.[21]

North Korea is also working to field the KN-08, a mobile ballistic missile capability, which produces a unique problem for the United States: if North Korean missile launchers can fire, move, and then quickly fire again from a different location, it stands to reason that U.S. intelligence assets may find it difficult to physically locate and target the missiles, leaving U.S. bases—and potentially U.S. territory—vulnerable.[22] In addition to North Korea's fixed missile sites, drone fleet, and road-mobile ballistic missile capability, there are some indications that the country may also be developing long-range sea-launched ballistic missiles.[23]

For more than two decades, the major debate in Korea policy circles was whether or not to engage with Pyongyang. That question, however, is becoming irrelevant; engagement can be useful for many reasons, but few credible experts believe it will disarm North Korea. Instead, the core question the United States and South Korea must eventually face is: Can we live with a North Korea that possesses a survivable nuclear force? If we cannot, what are we willing to do to prevent it? If we can, how will we mitigate the associated political and security risks?

---

[17] Wyatt Olson, "U.S. 'Strategic Patience' Policy toward North Korea Not Working, Analyst Says," *Stars and Stripes*, November 10, 2014.

[18] See, for example, Robert Gates, *Duty* (New York: Knopf, 2014).

[19] Brad Glosserman and David Santoro, "The 'Lynchpin' Grapples with Frustration and Distrust: The Fourth U.S.-ROK Strategic Dialogue," Pacific Forum CSIS, Issues & Insights, February 2012.

[20] Jackson, "Kim Jong Un's Tin Can Air Force."

[21] "NK's March Missile Test Aimed at Evading Interceptor Systems: Sources," *Yonhap*, June 19, 2014.

[22] John Barry, "The Defense Secretary's Exit Interview," *Daily Beast*, June 21, 2011.

[23] Julian Ryall, "North Korea Launches Soviet-Era Style Ballistic Missile Submarine," *Telegraph*, November 3, 2014.

What the United States Can Do

The United States is not, and must not be, a passive actor in Asia's changing security landscape. Each of the trends described above can be shaped, arrested, or otherwise leveraged in a way that keeps Asia stable and leaves future policymakers with better options than we face today.

The next phase in U.S. Asia strategy must nudge the region toward transparency in terms of operations, capabilities, and, to the extent possible, intentions as well. Gray zone coercion loses much of its efficacy in an environment rendered transparent. If a would-be aggressor knows it will be seen as such by its neighbors, that transparency may have the effect of deterring gray zone coercion. Even if not, the ability for Asian states to see aggression for what it is has the potential to galvanize cooperation to isolate an aggressor. Although it would involve many obstacles and could not be a panacea, two major initiatives can help move the region in the direction of greater transparency: the proliferation of operational level military engagement and cooperative maritime domain awareness.

Reciprocal engagement with militaries throughout the region—including China's and North Korea's military—may have the possible indirect benefit of socializing U.S. values and building U.S. ties to influential figures in foreign governments. More concretely, in many foreign governments, such as North Korea, military organizations hold disproportionate sway relative to other bureaucratic and political actors. Engaging them reduces the potential for communication distortions that may result from dealing with unreliable or parochial and self-interested interlocutors simply because of mirror imaging the U.S. system. The power of foreign ministries around the world—which traditionally manage engagement processes—varies greatly depending on the government. It makes little sense in today's increasingly interconnected world that embassies and foreign ministries serve as the only ties connecting governments. Military engagement can also communicate deterrence without ever having to make a threat. The U.S. military is impressive, and the ability for other militaries to see that up close can induce caution. Finally, and especially at the operational level, military engagement can help prevent the U.S. military from forming inaccurate biases about potential competitors' capabilities and intentions by directly exposing it to other militaries' operations and equipment. For military engagement to be an effective tool of statecraft, however, it must be more than symbolic, and there must be a degree of reciprocity.

The second initiative that can advance transparency in the region is the formation of a multilateral information-sharing regime often referred to as a Common Operating Picture (COP). At the risk of overstating its potential, a COP may be seen as a technological approach to ameliorating a political and security problem. At CNAS, we are researching the political, operational, and technical requirements that would allow participating nations to have greater awareness of what goes on in international waters, especially in high friction areas. Information-sharing regimes intended to increase operational transparency exist as a patchwork at the bilateral and trilateral level in Asia, and we believe that greater situational awareness—ideally in real-time—would benefit the region as a whole and increase the political costs of gray zone coercion or other forms of military adventurism. Furthermore, if everyone in Asia had a common picture of which actors were doing what and where, inadvertent friction could be better managed or avoided altogether.

To address Asia's military modernization, the optimal U.S. approach is not to try and disrupt the trend, but to steer it in a defensive direction. Doing that requires a U.S. strategy for how to leverage its security cooperation resources in a coherent and orchestrated way. If U.S. allies and partners are going to modernize their militaries no matter what, it makes sense to offer them modern equipment and training that favor defensive—rather than offensive—uses. For example, improved surveillance and reconnaissance equipment, coastal defense capabilities, land-based anti-ship cruise missiles, helicopters, ballistic missile defense systems, and undersea mines all represent examples of capabilities that can modernize a military in a way that improves territorial defenses and could even improve technical cooperation among Asian militaries without necessarily provoking the ire of militaries around the region.

Finally, to manage the North Korean nuclear threat, we must embrace the possibility of limited war and plan accordingly. The United States cannot reasonably be expected to capitulate to North Korean demands and simply recognize it as a nuclear power, nor should it launch a preventive war to disable North Korea's nuclear capability—at this point in time. The history of the modern Korean Peninsula suggests that some version of the status quo ante will continue to prevail; North Korea will likely continue to move toward securing an assured second-strike nuclear capability. While we should continue to encourage reconciliation between North and South Korea, and continue to engage North Korea ourselves to the extent possible, we must recognize that as long as our relationship with North Korea remains hostile, we have a responsibility to guard against the prospect of North Korean limited military campaigns. Some of North Korea's recent rhetoric suggests that possibility, as does the logic of a nuclear North Korea that believes it has secured a nuclear deterrent.

Thank you for this opportunity to appear before you. I look forward to answering your questions.

Mr. SALMON. Thank you. Mr. Goodman.

STATEMENT OF MR. MATTHEW P. GOODMAN, WILLIAM E. SIMON CHAIR IN POLITICAL ECONOMY, SENIOR ADVISER FOR ASIAN ECONOMICS, CENTER FOR STRATEGIC AND INTERNATIONAL STUDIES

Mr. GOODMAN. Thank you, Mr. Chairman, Mr. Ranking Member, distinguished members of the subcommittee. I'm delighted to have a chance to talk about the economic dimension of the rebalancing of our economic opportunities and challenges in this important region, Asia-Pacific.

As someone who works on economics in a foreign policy think tank, I sometimes joke that my colleagues work on life and liberty, and I work on the pursuit of happiness, and so that's the way I look at the economic story in Asia, because it's largely a positive one for us. So, I'd just like to make four points.

First, the economic stakes for the United States in the Asia-Pacific are enormous. The region accounts for around 60 percent of global GDP, includes eight of the world's $15 trillion economies, and it's consistently been the fastest growing region of the world in recent times. By 2030, Asia will likely be home to 3 billion middle class consumers, which is a huge opportunity for us to export American goods and services, beef, pork, soybeans, aircraft, software, healthcare services, and the many other things that we are competitive in. But U.S. economic engagement with Asia also comes with a number of challenges. We have sizable trade deficits, as Congressman Sherman mentioned, with a number of Asian countries. Our companies face an array of barriers and unfair trade practices both at and behind the border in many Asian economies from regulatory impediments, to theft of intellectual property. And excess savings; I'm a former Treasury guy, so I have to say excess savings in Asia create macroeconomic imbalances that can be destabilizing, as we saw in the global financial crisis; which leads to my second point.

Addressing these challenges and these opportunities, and maximizing these opportunities requires a robust U.S. economic diplomacy in the region. And, indeed, administrations of both parties over the past 40 years have pursued an active economic strategy toward Asia from Nixon's opening of China, which really facilitated China's reform and opening strategy, to the Obama administration's pursuit of the Trans-Pacific Partnership, which I'll come back to.

The basic objectives of U.S. economic strategy across these administrations have been threefold. The first is growth and jobs. Stronger demand, rising purchasing power, and lowering trade barriers means more opportunities for U.S. exporters, which translates into growth and jobs at home.

The second objective is upholding and updating the rules of the international economic order. Those rules have increasingly fallen out of step with the realities of today's global economy which revolves around integrated value chains. This means trade agreements need to be updated, not just to cover things that happen at the border like tariffs and other border measures, but also behind the border issues, like the behavior of state-owned enterprises, regulatory practices, intellectual property protection, and so forth.

Finally, U.S. economic policy in the Asia-Pacific has been aimed at underpinning America's long-term presence in the region. Our alliances with Japan, South Korea, Australia and others have provided long-term stability and security in the region, and these trade investment and other economic arrangements help provide a critical economic equivalent enmeshing the U.S. in regional affairs, and reassuring our allies and potential adversaries of our long-term commitment to the region.

My third point is that there is a new reality in Asia shaping our economic engagement, which is obviously the rise of China and India. I'll focus mainly on China. Just 15 years ago, China's economy was roughly one-ninth the size of ours. Today it is the world's second largest economy, and could surpass ours in nominal terms in just a few years.

China clearly has ambitions to resume its historical position as the Middle Kingdom at the heart of Asia, which has implications for the established order in the region and the U.S. role in it.

Not all of this is a bad thing. China's economic success has created a significant new source of demand for the United States and neighboring countries and, therefore, economic and export opportunities. Beijing has to date largely been a rule taker in the regional economic order, and has even been a constructive player in regional institutions such as APEC, but Beijing has also, of course, been selective in its compliance with international rules and norms, as others have mentioned; failing to honor the spirit of its WTO commitments, tilting the playing field in favor of its industrial champions, and harming the interests of U.S. companies.

Moreover, Beijing is clearly seeking a greater voice in setting international rules and standards, and imbuing them with Chinese characteristics, setting up new institutions that raise questions about the sustainability of the Bretton Woods institutions that we champion for so long. So, this means we have to have this robust economic strategy to deal with both these challenges and opportunities of interacting with China.

Final point is about TPP. It is obviously right now the sharp end of the spear of our economic engagement in Asia, and it serves all three of the enduring objectives that I mentioned of U.S. economic strategy in Asia, substantial economic gains, potentially, updating the rules of the regional trade with new disciplines in the areas I mentioned, and TPP would embed the U.S. more deeply in the Asia-Pacific region, and reassure our allies who are skeptical about our long-term commitment.

As you know, TPP is near the end game, and it's now believed this could be brought to you and Congress for consideration as soon as later this year. The stakes are very high. I think this is a critical component of the rebalance. Without the economic components, and TPP as the, as I say, the sharp end of the spear, then the rebalance is seen as a primarily military endeavor, and that's not going to be acceptable to the region, so we need to pursue this agreement for a number of reasons. Thank you very much.

[The prepared statement of Mr. Goodman follows:]

CSIS | CENTER FOR STRATEGIC & INTERNATIONAL STUDIES

Statement before the House Committee on Foreign Affairs

Subcommittee on Asia and the Pacific

"U.S. ECONOMIC OPPORTUNITIES AND CHALLENGES IN THE ASIA PACIFIC"

A Statement by:

Matthew P. Goodman

William E. Simon Chair in Political Economy

Center for Strategic and International Studies (CSIS)

February 26, 2015

2172 Rayburn House Office Building

Introduction

Mr. Chairman, Mr. Ranking Member, Members of the Subcommittee, thank you for this opportunity to offer my thoughts on U.S. economic opportunities and challenges in the Asia-Pacific region.

Economics is at the heart of American engagement in the Asia Pacific. Trade, investment, and other economic ties across the Pacific today are measured in the trillions of dollars and make an essential contribution to U.S. growth and jobs. No other region of the world presents as many opportunities and challenges for the U.S. economy—and for U.S. international economic policy.

Like administrations before it, the Obama Administration has put economics at the center of its Asia-Pacific strategy. Indeed, the overall success of the Administration's policy of "rebalancing" to Asia rests on its ability to carry out a successful economic strategy in the region, in particular completion of a high-standard Trans-Pacific Partnership (TPP) trade agreement.

Asia's Economic Gravity

The United States is drawn to the Asia Pacific by strong economic forces. In 2014, the 21 member economies of the Asia-Pacific Economic Cooperation (APEC) grouping, which includes the United States, accounted for 58 percent of global gross domestic product (GDP).[1] The region is home to the world's three largest economies by GDP – the United States, China, and Japan – and 8 of its 15 trillion-dollar economies. Moreover, the International Monetary Fund (IMF) projects that emerging and developing Asia will grow 6.4 percent in 2015, making it the world's fastest-growing region, as it has been consistently for nearly a decade.[2] By 2030, it is expected that Asia will be home to over three billion middle-class consumers, who will account for over 40 percent of global middle-class consumption.[3]

These trends will lead to increased international commerce in a region where trade is already substantial. Last year, more than $10 trillion in goods and services flowed around the Pacific, and the APEC region accounted for 44 percent of total global trade.[4] Six of America's top 10 trading partners are in APEC, and our exports to the grouping as a whole have more than doubled over the past decade. In 2013, APEC economies absorbed nearly 62 percent of total U.S. exports. As the region – and its middle class – continues to grow, this will lead to even greater

---

[1] White House Office of the Press Secretary, "Fact Sheet: 22nd Annual APEC Economic Leaders' Meeting," November 11, 2014, http://www.whitehouse.gov/the-press-office/2014/11/11/fact-sheet-22nd-annual-apec-economic-leaders-meeting. APEC is discussed further below as a centerpiece of U.S. regional economic strategy.

[2] International Monetary Fund, "January Update: Cross Currents," *World Economic Outlook,* January 2015, https://www.imf.org/external/pubs/ft/weo/2015/update/01/.

[3] David Rohde, "The Swelling Middle," January, 2012, http://www.reuters.com/middle-class-infographic. This figure includes India, and other Asian economies not members of APEC.

[4] White House Office of the Press Secretary, *op cit.*

demand for high-quality American goods and services, from our beef, pork, and soybeans, to our aircraft, software, and healthcare services.

We are also tied to the Asia Pacific through both direct and portfolio investment. The stock of U.S. direct investment in Asia on a historical-cost basis totaled almost $700 billion at the end of 2013, having grown by an average of more than $40 billion per year for the past half-decade.[5] Over the same period, investment from Asia-Pacific countries into the United States rose by almost $150 billion, adding to an accumulated stock that now totals more than $450 billion.[6] China and Japan each hold over $1 trillion in U.S. Treasury securities,[7] and Asians and Americans have trillions of dollars invested in each other's stock markets and other private financial instruments.

All of this economic activity across the Pacific means jobs at home. The International Trade Administration estimates that exports to Asia and the Pacific supported 3.2 million jobs across the United States in 2013, the largest share of any single region.[8] That same year, Asian companies invested in the United States directly employed nearly one million Americans, with many more jobs supported indirectly by these operations.[9]

In addition to the opportunities, we also face major policy challenges in our economic engagement with Asia. The United States continues to run large and persistent trade deficits with many Asian economies, including a $327 billion trade deficit with China in 2013.[10] While tariffs across the region have been lowered by an average of 10 percent since APEC's founding in 1989, American companies continue to face an array of barriers and unfair trade practices both at and behind the border in many Asian countries, from regulatory impediments to theft of intellectual property. Meanwhile, excess savings in many Asian economies, while supporting American consumption and the ability of the Federal government to borrow at low rates in the near term, contribute to macroeconomic imbalances that can be destabilizing over time. Currency manipulation by some countries in the region has exacerbated this problem.

---

[5] Bureau of Economic Analysis, "Balance of Payments and Direct Investment Position Data," U.S. Department of Commerce, http://www.bea.gov/iTable/index_MNC.cfm.
[6] Ibid.
[7] U.S. Department of the Treasury, "Major Foreign Holders of Treasury Securities," January 2015, http://www.treasury.gov/resource-center/data-chart-center/tic/Documents/mfh.txt.
[8] Chris Rasmussen and Elizabeth Schaefer, "Jobs Supported by Export Destination 2013," International Trade Administration, U.S. Department of Commerce, July 7, 2014, http://www.trade.gov/mas/ian/build/groups/public/@tg_ian/documents/webcontent/tg_ian_0053 72.pdf.
[9] Organization for International Investment, "Insourcing Facts," August 2012, http://www.ofii.org/resources/insourcing-facts. Estimate based on Asia's share of overall U.S. inbound FDI.
[10] Bureau of Economic Analysis, "International Transactions, International Services, and International Investment Position (IIP) Tables," U.S. Department of Commerce, http://www.bea.gov/iTable/index_ita.cfm.

Addressing these challenges and maximizing the economic opportunities that the Asia Pacific presents require a robust U.S. economic diplomacy in the region.

U.S. Economic Strategy in the Asia Pacific

The United States is a Pacific power, and economics has been intertwined with our diplomatic and security engagement in the region since the dawn of the republic. The first U.S. merchant ship set sail from New York bound for Canton in 1784, bearing ginseng, cotton, and lead to trade for Chinese tea, tableware, silk, and spice; it also carried the first U.S. consul to be stationed in China. In 1853, Commodore Matthew Perry arrived in Tokyo Bay in his "black ships" seeking open trade with Japan and refueling rights for the American whaling fleet.

Since the end of World War II, economics has played a vital role in underpinning the network of U.S. security alliances in the Asia Pacific. As the Cold War deepened, the United States first supported the revival of the Japanese, Korean, and Taiwanese economies as part of its efforts to develop durable bulwarks against the spread of communism. In 1972, the Nixon Administration engineered a dramatic opening to China, creating the opportunity for an explosive increase in economic engagement when the world's most populous country entered its period of "reform and opening" later that decade. The broad contours of this strategy of engagement have been upheld by every Republican and Democratic administration since.

Beginning in the late 1980s, bilateral economic engagement in the Asia Pacific has been complemented by efforts to promote regional economic integration. The APEC forum has been the organizing principle for these efforts. President George H.W. Bush's Secretary of State James Baker embraced an Australian proposal to create APEC in 1989 as a venue for foreign ministers from around the region to discuss trade and investment liberalization and capacity-building. The underlying logic of APEC was to channel the aspirations of East Asian countries for regional economic integration into a trans-Pacific framework that included the United States (as well as other Pacific-facing nations such as Canada, Mexico, Peru, and Chile). President Bill Clinton invited his APEC counterparts to a summit on Blake Island off Seattle in 1993, lending top-level political support to APEC's mission of regional economic integration.

APEC has also been at the heart of the Obama Administration's strategy of "rebalancing" to Asia. The rebalance has military, diplomatic, economic, and people-to-people components, each of which underpins and enhances the other elements. As discussed further below, the economic dimension of the rebalance centers on negotiation of a TPP trade agreement among a subset of APEC economies.

Over successive administrations, U.S. economic strategy in the Asia Pacific has been guided by three broad objectives. The first is growth and jobs. As discussed above, the Asia Pacific is the world's largest and fastest-growing economic area. Stronger demand and rising purchasing power in Asia means more opportunities for U.S. exporters, which translates into growth and jobs at home.

The second objective is upholding and updating the rules of the international economic order. Since World War II, Washington has championed an open, rules-based system of trade and investment, which has yielded enormous benefits for the United States and the rest of the world. However, the rules have grown increasingly out of step with the realities of today's global economy. They reflect a 19th century model of arms-length trade in goods, rather than 21st century phenomena such as e-commerce and integrated value chains. TPP is designed to address this gap by establishing updated rules governing not only tariffs and other border measures but also behind-the-border issues such as the market behavior of state-owned enterprises, regulatory transparency, labor and environmental standards, and intellectual property protection.

The third enduring objective of U.S. economic strategy in the Asia Pacific is supporting America's long-term presence in the region. The United States is a Pacific power but not an Asian nation. Thus successive administrations have worked to embed the United States in the region through a host of political, security, and economic arrangements, while opposing efforts that would "draw a line down the middle of the Pacific," in the words of former Secretary of State Baker. U.S. alliances with Japan, South Korea, Australia, and others, as well as the American troops and ships deployed across the region, are the most visible manifestation of this policy. Binding trade arrangements such as the U.S.-Korea free trade agreement (KORUS FTA) and TPP provide a crucial economic equivalent. They enmesh the United States in regional affairs, give Asia-Pacific countries an increased stake in each other's prosperity and security, and help reassure our allies and potential adversaries of Washington's continued commitment to robust engagement with the region.

A New Reality in Asia

The Obama Administration's rebalancing strategy is partly motivated by what is undoubtedly the single greatest trend shaping regional – and global – economic dynamics: China's rise. At the start of the 21st century, the Chinese economy was only one-quarter the size of the Japanese economy, and roughly one-ninth the size of the U.S. economy. Today, China is the world's second-largest economy, having passed Japan in 2010, and on current trends, it could reemerge as the largest economy in nominal terms as soon as 2021.[11] The rapidity of China's ascent, its latent potential as the world's most populous nation, and its ambitions to resume its historical position as the "Middle Kingdom" at the heart of Asia are challenging the established regional economic order.

To date Beijing has largely been a rule taker within the international economic order. It joined the World Trade Organization (WTO) in 2001, played a constructive role in the G20 during the early days of the global financial crisis, and has become deeply integrated within regional and global value chains. It supported a U.S. initiative in APEC in 2011 to lower member economies' tariffs on

---

[11] "Catching the eagle," *The Economist*, August 22, 2014,
http://www.economist.com/blogs/graphicdetail/2014/08/chinese-and-american-gdp-forecasts.

environmental goods and services. During its own host year in 2014, Beijing put forward an ambitious agenda for advancing trans-Pacific regional economic integration by pushing for faster progress towards a Free Trade Area of the Asia-Pacific (FTAAP)—another U.S.-proposed initiative. And, despite initially rejecting TPP as an effort by Washington to "contain" China, Beijing has shifted in recent years toward seeking a better understanding of the initiative. Through negotiations with the United States over a high-standard bilateral investment treaty (BIT), Beijing has even shown its own interest in preparing the ground for eventual participation in a high-standard trade agreement.

At the same time, China has been selective in its compliance with international economic rules and norms. It has failed to honor the spirit of many of its WTO commitments and continues to restrict the activities of U.S. companies in key sectors of American comparative advantage. Through an array of subsidies, regulatory barriers, and the uneven application of domestic laws, China has given preferential treatment to its firms over U.S. companies operating within its market – particularly in sectors it deems of strategic importance, such as high technology.[12] Lack of intellectual property protection, including cyber-theft of U.S. trade secrets, has been a persistent problem for American interests.

Moreover, under the Xi Jinping administration, Beijing is clearly seeking a greater voice in setting international rules and standards and imbuing them with "Chinese characteristics." To an extent, this is understandable: historically, China was at the center of the Asian economic order. Moreover, it is true that Beijing is underrepresented in many existing institutions of global economic governance. Its voting share in the IMF, for example, is roughly equivalent to the combined share of Belgium and the Netherlands – despite having an economy seven times their combined size.

But Beijing's growing assertiveness in international economic rule-making comes with certain risks. For example, through the Regional Comprehensive Economic Partnership (RCEP), an alternative trade arrangement to TPP bringing together 16 Asian countries, Beijing is advancing a lower-standards model of regional economic integration that could put American commercial interests at a disadvantage when competing in the region. Meanwhile, Beijing has championed new initiatives such as the Asian Infrastructure Investment Bank (AIIB) and the Silk Road Fund, in an effort to establish its centrality in the region's institutional architecture. These new institutions could weaken established rules and norms for best practices in development assistance – such as environmentally sound lending standards and protection of vulnerable populations – that the existing Bretton Woods institutions have developed over many decades.

---

[12] For one discussion of these issues, see Usha C. V. Haley and George T. Haley, *Subsidies to Chinese Industry: State Capitalism, Business Strategy, and Trade Policy*, Oxford University Press, April 25, 2013.

China's new position, policies, and ambitions in the Asia Pacific have raised the stakes for the United States to pursue a robust economic agenda in the region. This includes engaging with China directly to cooperate on issues of mutual concern, manage competition where necessary, and advance the full range of American interests in the region. It also means working with America's regional allies and partners to strengthen the rules-based order – including through initiatives like TPP – and to offer Beijing "carrots" to encourage constructive engagement and integration into the established order, and "sticks" to discourage zero-sum economic behavior.

The Trans-Pacific Partnership

As mentioned earlier, TPP is the centerpiece of the Obama Administration's rebalancing strategy to Asia. U.S. involvement in TPP dates to the waning days of the Bush Administration in late 2008, when the White House notified Congress of its intention to negotiate a trade agreement with four small APEC economies – Brunei, Chile, New Zealand, and Singapore. The Obama Administration formally embraced TPP in late 2009. Australia, Peru, and Vietnam joined the effort shortly thereafter, and negotiations among the eight original member countries began in March 2010. The initiative has since attracted four additional members: Malaysia later in 2010; Canada and Mexico in 2012; and Japan in the summer of 2013. Together the 12 TPP negotiating partners represent a combined 40 percent of the global economy by GDP and almost one-third of world exports.

TPP serves all three enduring objectives of U.S. economic strategy in Asia. First, it holds the promise of substantial economic gains. The Peterson Institute for International Economics has estimated $223.4 billion in annual global welfare gains from a concluded TPP in 2025, including $76.6 billion in GDP gains for the United States and a $123.5 billion increase in U.S. exports relative to the baseline scenario.[13]

Second, a completed TPP agreement would update the rules of regional trade. As President Obama said in announcing his support for the initiative, TPP is designed to produce "the high standards worthy of a 21st-century trade agreement."[14] In addition to lowering border barriers, a successful TPP will establish an array of behind-the-border rules to facilitate regional trade and investment, including disciplines on state-owned enterprises, high labor and environment standards, strengthened intellectual property protections, and more transparent regulation. Moreover, TPP's open architecture will allow it to incorporate new members after its conclusion, strengthening its potential as a driver and *de facto* template for a new multilateral system of rules.

---

[13] From Peter A. Petri, Michael G. Plummer, Fan Zhai, *The Trans-Pacific Partnership and Asia-Pacific Integration: A Quantitative Assessment,* Peterson Institute for International Economics and East-West Center, Updated May, 2013, http://asiapacifictrade.org/wp-content/uploads/2013/05/Adding-Japan-and-Korea-to-TPP.pdf.
[14] White House, "Remarks by President Barack Obama at Suntory Hall," news release, November 14, 2009, www.whitehouse.gov/the-press-office/remarks-president-barack-obama-suntory-hall

A new high-standard regime would have positive effects for U.S. economic and commercial interests, positive spillover effects for our allies and partners in the region, and create new incentives for countries to seek to upgrade their own standards. This includes China, which, as an APEC member, is theoretically eligible for eventual TPP participation. However, the standards of the agreement, such as the aforementioned disciplines on state-owned enterprises, are designed to ensure that if China were to join TPP, it would have to offer strong and enforceable guarantees of a fair and level playing field in its domestic market.

Third, TPP would embed the United States more deeply in the Asia-Pacific region and reinvigorate American leadership there. It would strengthen trade and investment ties across the Pacific and deepen regional economic integration. It would also demonstrate a long-term American commitment to the region that complements our security presence there. Our Asian partners want the U.S. military to remain as a source of stability in the region, but they do not want only that; they also seek our markets, capital, ideas, and leadership in championing the economic rules of the road.

By all accounts, TPP is entering the endgame. The United States and Japan are reportedly close to agreement on a bilateral market-access deal that is widely considered a precondition to a broader deal among the 12 parties. TPP chief negotiators will meet early next month in an effort to prepare the ground for a potentially decisive meeting of TPP ministers in mid-April. There is now an emerging consensus among trade analysts that a final TPP deal can be completed and brought to Congress for a vote before the end of this year.

The stakes could not be higher for the Obama Administration. Conclusion of TPP is the *sine qua non* of success not only for the Administration's regional economic policy but arguably for the entire Asia rebalancing strategy, insofar as it is a necessary complement to the U.S. security and diplomatic presence in the region.

Conclusion

America's interests in the Asia Pacific are broad, deep, and enduring. None is more important than our economic stake in the region. As former Secretary of State Hillary Clinton explained in laying out the rationale for the rebalancing strategy in 2011, "Harnessing Asia's growth and dynamism is central to American economic and strategic interests and a key priority for President Obama. Open markets in Asia provide the United States with unprecedented opportunities for investment, trade, and access to cutting-edge technology. Our economic recovery at home will depend on exports and the ability of American firms to tap into the vast and growing consumer base of Asia."[15]

A successful economic strategy in the Asia Pacific is essential to sustaining American growth and jobs into the 21st century. It is also central to Washington's

---

[15] Hillary Clinton, "America's Pacific Century," *Foreign Policy*, October 11, 2011, http://foreignpolicy.com/2011/10/11/americas-pacific-century.

efforts to remain a champion of the global rules-based order. And it underpins America's long-term presence in the region, which in turn contributes importantly to the region's security and prosperity.

Thank you for your attention.

———

Mr. SALMON. Thank you. Mr. Denmark.

STATEMENT OF MR. ABRAHAM M. DENMARK, SENIOR VICE PRESIDENT, POLITICAL AND SECURITY AFFAIRS AND EXTERNAL RELATIONS, THE NATIONAL BUREAU OF ASIAN RESEARCH

Mr. DENMARK. Thank you very much, Mr. Chairman, Mr. Ranking Member, and the distinguished members of the subcommittee.

I agree with the ranking member that when we talk about Asia, we have so many issues and so little time. And since my time is ticking away rapidly, I'm going to just focus on three things, and look forward to our conversation later.

The first is looking at China. As has been mentioned before, the rise of China is probably the most significant and profound geopolitical trend of the 21st century. Its economic rise, its rapid and profound military modernization program is really historically unprecedented, and something that is of tremendous importance to American interests. But the rising prosperity that China has experienced in recent years is forcing Beijing to adjust to the demands of a modern economy and rising expectations of its people.

China is facing unprecedented levels of urbanization, privatization, marketization, globalization, and what they call informatization. It speeds in scale that we've really never seen before. This economic development is creating corruption, environmental degradation, social dislocation, economic disparity, and political unrest that is incredibly challenging for Beijing to manage.

These are challenges that Beijing is very much aware of. These are Beijing's absolute top priorities, and China's leaders are engaging on several programs to address them; the most well known being Xi Jinping's anti-corruption campaign. And this is a very serious campaign that Beijing is going through; tens of thousands of senior cadres have already been charged with corruption, hundreds of thousands of lower level officials have been charged with corruption, and the Bank of America has estimated that China's GDP fell by 1.5 percent last year solely as the result of government officials no longer buying luxury goods and real estate, so this is a huge problem, but also a major program that Beijing is going through. It has important implications for the rule of—for Xi Jinping's power, and for Chinese politics. And it informs Beijing's ability to craft its approach to foreign policy and U.S.-China relations.

I would argue that in the grand scheme of things, China is not pursing a radically revisionist agenda in the international system, and that it sees that it is this system that allowed it to grow prosperous, to remain stable. Where China is revisionist, however, is regionally. As has been said before, China is attempting to establish something what I call a neo-tributary system which places it at the center of the Asia-Pacific's economic, political, and security destiny; a destiny that in China's mind does not include the United States playing a major role. This is, obviously, something that is very problematic for American interests, and so we are engaging them in a wide variety of different activities that involve both cooperation and competition.

The second issue I wanted to address with you has been brought up a little bit already, is American alliances and partnerships in the Asia-Pacific. Our alliances are absolutely critical to American interests going forward. They are at the center of our power, our influence, and our presence in the region, and something that we need to be able to maintain and update for the requirements of the 21st century.

Japan is, obviously, a very important alliance for the United States. Prime Minister Abe is revitalizing Japan's economy, but also revitalizing the role that Japan can play in the geopolitical realm in the Asia-Pacific. By working with us on new defense program guidelines, we have a tremendous opportunity to bolster their capabilities, and find a new capable and more balanced alliance that will help our interests, help maintain stability in the region.

It has also been mentioned that India is incredibly important to the United States. President Obama is the first American President to be invited to India to celebrate Republic Day. He's also the first President to visit India twice while in office. Prime Minister Modi clearly sees the United States as incredibly important to India's interests, and there are great opportunities for us to engage with them strategically, politically, and economically. India's ACDIS policy has tremendous potential complementarities with our rebalancing policy, and I think those are complementarities that we need to address.

Third and finally, there's been a lot of questions and lot of ink spilled over questions about the long-term potential for American power. Many in Asia, some in the United States talk about potential American decline, that we are going to be overshadowed by the rise of China, the rise of other powers in Asia. And I actually wanted to make the point here that I think this is a very wrong analysis. I actually think that the United States has tremendous potential to remain powerful and dominant in the Asia-Pacific. Our economy is the most rigorous, the most powerful in the region, our military is the most powerful in the region. The key for us, though, is to take this potential and translate it into actual power. We have opportunities to maintain our power and dominance in the region, but it's going to require the adroit leadership and good decision making from our leaders in the Executive Branch, and from you all in Congress.

I look forward to talking with you about U.S. strategy and dynamics in the Asia-Pacific. Thank you very much.

[The prepared statement of Mr. Denmark follows:]

Prepared Testimony by

Abraham M. Denmark
Senior Vice President
The National Bureau of Asian Research

to the

House Committee on Foreign Affairs
Subcommittee on Asia and the Pacific

Subject: "Across the Other Pond:
U.S. Opportunities and Challenges in the Asia Pacific"

February 26, 2015

Good morning, Mr. Chairman and Members of the Subcommittee.

Thank you for inviting me to testify on U.S. opportunities and challenges in the Asia-Pacific. The region is of vital importance to our interests today, and the issues we face are both profound and complex. How the United States positions itself to engage the region will have significant implications for our national destiny.

As the Asia-Pacific century unfolds and increasingly defines the contours of the new international environment, the United States must deepen its strategic engagement and leadership role in the region. Recent developments in the Asia-Pacific will have profound implications for the long-term power and influence of the United States. Following is an examination of several key political issues that will have significant implications for American foreign and national security policies toward the Asia-Pacific.

CHINA: INTERNAL POLITICS AND FOREIGN AFFAIRS

The rise of China is perhaps the most geopolitically significant trend of the 21st century. From Maoist collectivism, China has emerged as an economic powerhouse with burgeoning political influence and rapidly expanding military capabilities. While China's economic development since the late 1970s has been truly remarkable, and has benefitted hundreds of millions of Chinese people, its continuation is far from assured.

Rising prosperity has forced China to adjust to the demands of a modern economy and the rising expectations of its people. Economic development has resulted in urbanization, privatization, marketization, globalization, and "informatization" at a speed and scale that is historically unprecedented. Such rapid and monumental change has created several persistent challenges for Chinese society, including corruption, environmental degradation, social dislocation, economic disparity, and political unrest. Further, the decades-old one-child policy has created a monumental demographic problem in China, whose population is growing older and (sadly) possesses a disproportionate number of males.

All told, these issues threaten to undermine the fundamental legitimacy of the Chinese Communist Party (CCP) in the eyes of the Chinese people. CCP General Secretary Xi Jinping appears to be well aware of these challenges and is attempting to address them. The eminent scholar of elite Chinese politics Robert MacFarquhar argues that Xi is a Leninist but not a Marxist – a telling analysis in that it identifies

Xi's motivations to be more political than ideological. Xi's primary objective appears to be improving the Party, enhancing its ability to govern, and restoring its legitimacy. While he has advocated for initiatives to rebalance China's economy and enhance environmental protections, Xi's primary focus has been on combatting the rampant corruption that has long undermined Beijing's ability to adapt, evolve, and govern effectively.

Chairman Mao memorably advised that a worthy and charismatic leader "should not be obstructed by evil circumstances: he should dare to fight with heaven, struggle against the earth and cross swords with men." CCP General Secretary Xi Jinping seems to have taken this advice to heart and is engaged in a major anti-corruption campaign that has already had substantial effects on China's politics. The Bank of America estimates that China's GDP fell 1.5% last year solely as a result of government officials no longer purchasing luxury goods and real estate. The Central Commission for Discipline Inspection (CCDI) claims that it has initiated cases against 68 high-level officials and punished more than 70,000 officials for corruption, and it is estimated that more than 200,000 lower-level officials have been targeted for corruption. This effort has not spared some of China's most senior officials, including former domestic security tsar Zhou Yongkang, former vice chairman of the Central Military Commission General Xu Caihou, and Ling Jihua, top aide to former Secretary General Hu Jintao.

By taking on such prominent and high-level officials (as well as thousands of others at lower ranks), Xi has sent a message that no one is exempt from investigation and punishment for corruption. Although corruption is not the only problem that China's leaders face, Xi's ability to address other challenges will nevertheless be determined by his political clout. The anti-corruption campaign thus may help ensure that cadres are deterred from stymieing Xi's policy priorities.

It should be noted that anti-corruption and anti-pollution initiatives are not the only tool that Xi is using to bolster the Party's legitimacy. Other tools are at play as well – this is why China in recent years has intensified domestic intelligence and security efforts to a degree that are unprecedented for a China in the age of the Internet. Recently, technologies like virtual private networks (VPNs) – which popularly used to access foreign websites – have been blocked, whereas they had previously been tolerated.

Beijing has also intensified its use of nationalism as a way to bolster the Party's legitimacy. By emphasizing historical and territorial grievances with Japan and some of its other neighbors, the Party is able to justify itself as the only organization able to keep China unified, strong, and free from foreign exploitation. Officials in Beijing often express a reluctance to be seen as backing down on issues related to historical grievances or territorial claims, out of fear of criticism from high-level officials or patriotic "netizens."

For the foreseeable future, China's leaders are primarily focused on domestic affairs. Even though China's system is undemocratic and Leninist in structure, it should not be mistaken for being monolithic in any way. Individuals and organizations develop their own points of view, their own priorities, and their own strategies for achieving them. The competition between these groups and individuals makes for a politics that is both opaque and difficult to predict. China's political destiny will therefore remain as unclear as Beijing's skyline.

Foreign Policy and National Security Strategy

As China's power has grown, Beijing's approach to foreign policy and national security has evinced a greater level of confidence by its leaders. Whereas China had formerly sought to allay regional concerns about the implications of its rise by promoting the "peaceful rise" theory, Beijing has recently demonstrated a greater willingness to antagonize its neighbors in the pursuit of maritime claims over disputed waters and land features in the East and South China Seas. Today, most of China's maritime neighbors, including Japan, South Korea, Malaysia, Vietnam, the Philippines, and Indonesia, have expressed some level of concern about China's claims and the assertive tactics it has employed to enforce them.

As China has grown more prosperous, it has invested significant portions of that newfound wealth into developing its military. With defense budgets rising at a remarkable rate for decades, the People's Liberation Army (PLA) has rapidly evolved from one that was referred to as an "army of millet and rifles" to one that is increasingly capable and technologically sophisticated. Since the PLA does not have global responsibilities, China has been able to tailor its military modernization program to a relatively small set of possible contingencies, many of which call upon the PLA to deter and deny the ability of the U.S. military to intervene in crises or conflicts along China's periphery.

The PLA has traditionally focused its modernization program on Taiwan-related contingencies. This drove the development of advanced fighters, highly capable ships and submarines, and precise long-range missiles – all designed to complicate and raise the costs of a U.S. intervention during a Taiwan-related crisis. As relations between Beijing and Taipei have improved, other contingencies – primarily revolving around the East and South China Seas – appear to have become more prominent in Chinese contingency planning.

China has also sought to enhance its economic ties with the region by promoting regional trade and financial arrangements like the BRICS Bank, the Asia Infrastructure Investment Bank, the Regional Comprehensive Economic Partnership, the Silk Road Economic Belt, and the 21st Century Maritime Silk Road. While the exact parameters of many of these initiatives remain unclear, they reflect a frustration from Beijing with the inability of the international community (and especially the United States) to reform key Breton Woods institutions, such as the IMF. By not reforming these key institutions to reflect present-day realities, the United States is effectively driving China and other countries to find alternatives.

Less is known, however, about the broader geopolitical vision that these initiatives are designed to support. Many question whether Beijing will grow to support the international order or seek to revise it according to China's own particular interests. While these questions remain unanswered, the general contours of a grand strategy have emerged in recent years.

As former chairman of the National Intelligence Council Dr. Thomas Fingar has noted, Beijing appears to view the international system in fairly mixed terms. China has benefited greatly from the stability and free trade that the existing international order has provided. In some circumstances—usually defined by Beijing's evolving understanding of Chinese national interests—China's initial refusal to accede to such rules has gradually given way to accession.

On the other hand, Beijing demonstrates concerns that the existing international system could constrain Chinese actions and enable other nations to act counter to Chinese interests. They generally see the existing order as established and sustained by an American power often seen as fundamentally hostile to the rise of China. In the minds of many in Beijing, China's dependence on this order makes it dependent on the United States—an unacceptable arrangement, considering what they see as America's determination to prevent China from assuming its "proper" place in the global order.

When discussing the international order itself, Chinese scholars and officials often object to its unipolar quality and call for it to be revised to be "more democratic" by giving added weight to emerging powers. Specifically, China's objections to the global order seem to be primarily focused on objections to American preeminence itself.

Although still not detailed, recent statements by Chinese leaders suggest the outlines of a Chinese vision for revising the global order. At the heart of this apparent vision is a revitalized China that is stable and prosperous at home, is the dominant power in the Asia-Pacific, and is able to shape events around the world through a kind of neo-tributary system. Chinese leaders do not appear to see this vision as a coercive arrangement; rather, they paint this system as founded upon tight economic integration and the eventual recognition of China as the dominant regional power on which other states depend.

President Xi recently presented the outlines of some aspects of this vision to a summit of the Conference on Interaction Confidence-Building Measures in Asia (CICA) in May 2014. He challenged the United States' continued leadership role in Asia, declaring his opposition to stronger military alliances in the region and arguing that "security problems in Asia should eventually be solved by Asians themselves."

Taken as a whole, President Xi seems to envision an international system in which China's geopolitical power is widely represented and respected. Beyond that, for the foreseeable future China is comfortable with largely free-riding globally while seeking revisionism regionally along the lines of its own interests. Beijing seeks a region in which American power and freedom of action in the Asia-Pacific are limited, in which American alliances are weakened or dismantled, and in which China sits at the heart of the regional economic, security, and political order. International institutions and laws would only be applied or utilized when they are seen to be supportive of Chinese national interests; otherwise, they would be disregarded or only given lip service. To this end, China has sought to promote institutions such as the Asian Infrastructure Investment Bank and the Shanghai Cooperation Organization that may serve as alternatives to more established international institutions, while also promoting initiatives that support China's national interests.

How successful Xi will be in achieving this vision remains to be seen. So far, however, China has not been able to successfully establish anything resembling a geopolitical sphere of influence. While the economies of East Asia are closely intertwined with China, this has not translated into the kind of political influence that Beijing has sought. Indeed, it seems that countries most dependent on China economically are some of those most concerned about Chinese assertiveness. It seems that China's assertiveness has backfired; rather than coercing smaller nations into acquiescence, it has driven them to seek closer relations with the United States. A comparison of the robust and diverse network of alliances and partnerships that the United States enjoys with the complicated and antagonistic relations that China has with most of its neighbors clearly demonstrates the difficult that Beijing has had in establishing anything remotely resembling a sphere of influence.

U.S.-China Relations

Washington and Beijing continue to struggle to find mechanisms and language that accurately define the realities and the aspirations of their bilateral relationship. The most recent formulation – the pursuit of a new model of major power relations – was designed to recognize the importance of the bilateral relationship to both sides, as well as to provide a conceptual framework in which the two sides could address issues of mutual concern and manage areas of tension.

Both countries approach the relationship from a position of uncertainty and distrust. Beijing appears to be concerned that the United States is fundamentally opposed to China's rise and will seek out ways to constrain Chinese power. Washington, for its part, is concerned that China seeks to displace the United States as the dominant power in the Asia-Pacific and establish itself at the center of regional geopolitics. While such suspicions are unlikely to disappear for the foreseeable future, they should not preclude either side's ability to pursue a robust and effective relationship.

Ultimately, both the United States and China appear to be interested in finding ways to cooperate on issues of mutual interest and concern and to develop mechanisms to manage tensions. In terms increasing cooperation, issues such as climate change, counter-terrorism, and counter-proliferation seem to be the most likely for success. Indeed, presidents Obama and Xi during their last meeting agreed to pursue cooperation on addressing climate change – a promising development considering that China and the United States produce 45% of the world's greenhouse gases. In terms of managing tensions, incidents at sea, problems in cyberspace, and the possibility of instability on the Korean Peninsula are the most likely sources of crisis and thus should be at the top of the bilateral agenda.

Overall, U.S.-China relations will grow increasingly complex in the coming years. The relationship will include elements of cooperation and competition, and the specter of crisis and conflict will be ever-present. Those who claim that the United States and China are headed for a new Cold War fundamentally misread the nature of the relationship – our economies are closely interwoven, both sides seek positive relations with the other, neither side seeks to abolish the other, and the ideological disagreements that characterize U.S.-China relations do not nearly rise to the nature and tenor of ideological incompatibility that defined the Cold War. Instead, China and the United States appear to be headed for an era of prolonged geopolitical competition, in which both sides seek advantage across all measures of national power. Tension and crisis are likely, but mutual interests in stability and continued economic development will (hopefully) reduce the potential for outright conflict.

Hong Kong

The recent unrest in Hong Kong has shined an unwelcome spotlight on China. Beijing's decision to require a review of officials elected as chief executive violated the spirit of the Basic Law and the "one country, two systems" approach that supposedly guaranteed Hong Kong a great degree of political autonomy. The protests that resulted from that decision and captivated the world's attention demonstrated that the people of Hong Kong hold their political freedoms dear. China's actions clearly showed a lack of respect for democratic governance and Hong Kong's autonomy, and the implications of this event will echo for years to come.

While Beijing attempted to portray the protesters as a small minority of misguided people controlled by hostile foreign agitators, the real long-lasting implications of these events will primarily flow from Beijing's actions. The values and institutions that were at the foundation of Hong Kong's prosperity and special place in the world—independent courts, a free press, political autonomy, and legitimate law enforcement—have been severely damaged. A significant number of people in Hong Kong demonstrated their willingness to stand up against what they saw as China's efforts to influence Hong Kong's politics, and that political impetus has not disappeared. China's actions may have preserved its control over Hong Kong, but at the likely cost of alienation, political unrest, and persistent calls for autonomy and political freedom.

Moreover, the events of the past year in Hong Kong will reverberate elsewhere, especially in Taiwan. Since China seeks to unify Taiwan under a "one country, two systems" model similar to Hong Kong's, Beijing's seeming unwillingness to respect Hong Kong's autonomy will likely raise concerns that Taiwan would receive similar treatment. Taiwan is facing another political transition in 2016, and this will likely be a major issue of contention.

NORTH KOREA: BELLIGERENCE AND UNCERTAINTY

North Korea represents the most likely source of instability in East Asia. Its continued belligerence and brinkmanship, along with its ongoing nuclear weapons and ballistic missile programs, represent a profound challenge for regional stability and a major threat to the United States and our allies. North Korea's ongoing human rights abuses – as detailed in a landmark study from the United Nations – make the regime an insult to any conception of human rights. And finally, the violent and mercurial rule of Kim Jong-un emphasizes that North Korea remains as dangerous as ever.

When Kim Jong-un took power in 2011, many thought that his control of the state would be rather tenuous and short-lived. Yet in the intervening years, Kim appears to have been able to somewhat consolidate his authority. Thousands of senior cadres have reportedly been purged from leadership, replaced by junior officials who owe their positions to Kim directly. First guardian Ri Yong-ho was purged in July 2012, and Kim's uncle and mentor Jang Song-thaek was executed in 2013 for forming his own center of power and refusing to accept Kim's absolute rule. With the death of his aunt Kim Kyong-hui from a stroke the following year, the guardian system established by Kim Jong-il has been entirely dismantled.

This is not to say that Kim's rule is fully consolidated and stable. Indeed, even undisputed leaders of the world's most totalitarian systems (Mao and Kim Il-sung, for example) had to constantly guard against challenges to their authority, coups, and factionalization. Indeed, a cursory examination of other authoritarian regimes (the Soviet Union, Egypt, and Libya, for example) suggests that regimes that seem stable for decades can suddenly lose their authority and collapse. Even though the Kim family regime has survived through decades of repression, famine, and isolation, there is no reason to believe it can continue this way indefinitely. Suffice it to say that, for Pyongyang, past performance is not an indication of future results.

There are indeed indications that Kim Jong-un seems to lack the legitimacy of his father, and especially of his grandfather. His youth and inexperience have reportedly raised hackles from North Korean elites, and there are reports of political conversations and even protests roiling across North Korea. While Kim has been able to purge former cadres and install loyalists in their place, it is clear that he is under pressure to perform.

To date, North Korea's international behavior has not deviated significantly from past precedents. Pyongyang still uses a mix of apocalyptic threats and positive messaging, although it seems to be more willing to use these tactics in relatively quick succession rather than alternating between them over a period of months. Pyongyang's approach to nuclear weapons appears to be unchanged. Finally, while the recent cyber attacks on Sony in apparent retaliation for the film *The Interview* demonstrates that North Korea is able to utilize relatively new technologies for their own end, there is little indication that North Korea's cyber capabilities are all that sophisticated or represent a unique national security threat.

A significant shift, however, may be taking place in North Korea's foreign affairs. Kim has been repeatedly shunned by Xi Jinping, who has yet to meet with Kim even as he has upgraded China's engagement with South Korea. As Beijing seems to be emphasizing Seoul above Pyongyang as a strategic priority, North Korea apparently sees Russia as a viable alternative. The North Korean Foreign Ministry announced plans to "deepen political, economic and military contacts and exchanges" this year. This is following the launch of new economic projects and initiatives to expand transportation and investment. Last year, more senior North Korean leaders visited Russia than any other country, and Kim and Putin are reportedly planning to visit one another in the near future. This would make Putin the first foreign leader to visit Kim since he took power, and would help burnish Kim's legitimacy as a leader of standing equal to Putin's.

Ultimately, North Korea is not likely to deviate from its long-established role as regional pariah and bad actor. While efforts to engage Pyongyang should not be forestalled, optimism for positive progress should be excised from all expectations. For the foreseeable future, North Korea will represent a profound threat to the United States and our allies in East Asia, as well as to regional stability writ large. Its politics will likely remain opaque, and the long-term survivability of the regime will likely remain in doubt.

ENHANCING ALLIANCES AND PARTNERSHIPS

As the United States continues to rebalance toward the Asia-Pacific, alliances and partnerships will take on a greater significance in this strategy. They are already absolutely central to U.S. power, presence, and influence in the Asia-Pacific and around the world. We are fortunate to have such a broad, diverse, and robust network of alliance and partner relationships; no other country enjoys anything even remotely comparable to this system. They host tens of thousands of American military and civilian personnel, which enables the United States to truly act as a global superpower that keeps the peace while also allowing Washington to focus on more immediate crises. Indeed, while some scholars and officials lament that a seemingly unending series of crises will somehow undermine U.S. intentions to rebalance, the reality is that alliances have a profoundly additive quality to American power. Not only do they enable America's global presence; they also free Washington to focus on and address immediate crises (while often contributing to these efforts as well) and help preserve stability in the meantime.

Yet the fundamental nature of alliance and partner relations is going to shift in a rather dramatic fashion. Initially conceived as military relationships required by the geopolitical realities of World War I, World War II, and the Cold War, alliances for much of the 20th century were relatively straightforward arrangements. Uniform mechanisms for alliance management, such as NATO, were put in place to enable robust military coordination and cooperation against a shared existential foe. Economic ties naturally flowed from these relationships, as trade between the belligerent sides during the World Wars and Cold War was virtually nonexistent. Political coordination, though certainly more complicated, was also facilitated by this shared sense of multinational purpose and the "long twilight struggle" against a shared arch nemesis.

Asia in the 21st century looks nothing like Europe in the 20th. While the United States enjoys strong alliance relationships across the region, there is no mechanism like NATO to bring them together. Moreover, the economies of America's allies are tightly integrated with China – a dynamic that raises complicated strategic calculations for allies whose economic and strategic loyalties are increasingly divergent. Finally, political calculations among America's Asian allies are far more complicated than they were in Europe. Antagonism and distrust over past aggression continue to roil relations between Japan and South Korea, for example, which have not been able to find a way to move beyond their past the way France and Germany have.

Even the term "alliance" is growing more complicated for American strategy in the Asia-Pacific. While the United States has five formal treaty allies in Asia (Australia, Japan, the Philippines, South Korea, and Thailand), it also has robust partnership relations with a host of other Asian powers, such as India, Indonesia, New Zealand, Singapore, Vietnam, and (unofficially) Taiwan. Since pursuing a rebalancing strategy, the United States has recognized the geopolitical importance of strengthening its relationships with these nations and has consequently intensified its outreach.

As part of rebalancing, the United States has sought to upgrade its alliances and partnerships for the 21st century with a series of political, economic, and military initiatives. These initiatives – which include joining the East Asia Summit, reinvigorating efforts to conclude a Trans-Pacific Partnership (TPP) economic agreement, and upgrading military arrangements with several countries around the region – signal that alliances and partnerships are evolving from relationships based primarily on military arrangements to robust platforms that support political, economic, and military cooperation and coordination.

JAPAN: REINVIGORATION AND A CHANGING NATIONAL SECURITY STRATEGY

This year represents the 70th anniversary of the end of World War II. While Japan quickly emerged from the devastation of war to become one of the most vibrant and innovative economies in the world, recent decades have been defined by stagnation. Yet today Japan is in the midst of a profound reevaluation of its foreign, economic, and national security policies. Prime Minister Shinzo Abe seeks to bring Japan into the 21st century by reinvigorating Japan's economy, enhancing its self-defense capabilities, and buttressing its role in regional and global geopolitics.

Abe's "three arrows" strategy seeks to reinvigorate Japan's long-stagnant economy with a mix of fiscal stimulus, monetary easing, and structural reform. This strategy, dubbed "Abenomics," was characterized by the *Economist* as a "mix of reflation, government spending and a growth strategy designed to jolt the economy out of suspended animation that has gripped it for more than two decades." While Abe has had mixed results to date, many in Tokyo see Japan's joining the TPP as an important mechanism that could force structural and economic policy reforms that are necessary for the country's economic revitalization.

In the security sphere, Abe's Cabinet in July of 2014 approved his proposal to reinterpret Japan's constitution to end the ban on allowing Japanese military forces to exercise the right of collective self-defense. The move widens the set of options available to Japan's Self-Defense Forces and opens new opportunities for Japan to enhance its security relationships with the United States and other friendly nations.

It thus will have important implications for the U.S.-Japan alliance. Yet despite what some critics have claimed, this decision does not represent a rearmament or remilitarization of Japan. Several significant restrictions remain in place, as does Japan's pacifist constitution.

What ending the ban on collective self-defense enables is for Japan to play a more significant role in the Asia-Pacific as a security actor, and especially as an American ally. In October 2013 the two sides agreed to revise the bilateral defense guidelines, with the aim of being "full partners in a more balanced and effective alliance in which our two countries can jointly and ably rise to meet the regional and global challenges of the 21st century, by investing in cutting-edge capabilities, improving interoperability, modernizing force structure, and adapting alliance roles and missions to meet contemporary and future security realities."

Enhancing the U.S.-Japan alliance is of tremendous importance to American interests in the Asia-Pacific. A closer security arrangement will both enhance Japan's ability to play a more significant role in maintaining regional stability and allow for a tighter integration of American and Japanese forces during a conflict. Ultimately, efforts to enhance the alliance will increase the security and influence of the United States, buttress regional stability, and improve our ability to defend our allies and vital interests in the Asia-Pacific.

Unfortunately, Prime Minister Abe's efforts to reinvigorate Japan have been accompanied by an apparent instinct to raise questions about Japan's troubled history. While Abe (to his credit) has not sought to revise or deny any of Japan's apologies for past abuses, certain statements by Abe and other officials suggest that they would prefer to overlook or downplay the significance of some of Japan's worst behavior during the 20th century. This is unfortunate, unnecessary, and damaging to Japan's status and image across the Asia-Pacific. With Abe likely to visit the United States later this year to commemorate the end of World War II, this is an excellent opportunity for him to definitively and clearly explain his view of Japan's history as well as his vision for the future.

INDIA

The United States and India have a historic opportunity to dramatically enhance their bilateral relationship. President Obama is the first American president to be invited to India to celebrate Republic Day, and he became the first president to visit India twice while in office. This reflects Prime Minister Modi's enthusiasm for engaging the United States, as well as President Obama's commitment to set a robust agenda with India.

Strategically, Indian and American geopolitical objectives are beginning to converge. Most importantly, India's "Act East" strategy has the potential to find multiple complementarities with America's strategic rebalancing, as both sides emphasize the need for greater engagement with East Asia utilizing all elements of national power. With both sides seeking to enhance their presence and influence in the region, and both sides sharing important geopolitical interests, the opportunities for strategic cooperation and coordination are significant.

This is not to say that disagreements can be papered over. Fundamental differences over issues such as climate change and the ideal state of the international system will likely persist for the foreseeable future. Significant disparities in national power remain, and both sides have different policy preferences and priorities on several major issues. Nevertheless, the two sides share profound interests in some very important areas – agreements that have the potential to form the basis for a robust strategic partnership.

Modi has made it clear that he seeks to enhance relations with all of Asia's major powers. He has engaged Xi Jinping and Vladimir Putin directly, and has sought to maintain positive relations between their respective countries. This is understandable, as it is in India's interests to maintain generally positive and productive relations with China and Russia.

Yet beneath the surface, it is clear that Modi sees India's relations with the United States and our allies as being of particular strategic value. His engagements with his American, Japanese, and Australian counterparts have been particularly positive and substantive. While this is partially the result of shared democratic values, one foreign policy issue is by far the most decisive in drawing India closer to the United States and its allies: a shared concern for China and its increasingly assertive approach to the Asia-Pacific.

Modi's concerns about a rising China are entirely understandable, given that China and India have a long-standing border dispute that already triggered one war. The status of the Dalai Lama also remains a sensitive issue in their bilateral relationship. Moreover, many in New Delhi see a China with the ability to dominate East Asia as an anathema to India's long-term interests, and they are thus pursuing policies designed to enhance India's ability to check Chinese power. In this regard, the

United States offers an attractive option for New Delhi. It is a reliable balance to Chinese influence, and can help promote economic and political cohesiveness in the Asia-Pacific. More concretely, India sees the United States as an important potential source of investment and new technologies – both of which will be essential to managing its rapidly growing population and addressing its intensifying security requirements.

To make progress in their bilateral relationship, both India and the United States will have to take some difficult steps. First should be efforts on both sides to enhance economic engagement and interaction between the two economies. Enhancing bilateral investment and trade will add a significant ballast to the relationship, and help create large constituencies on both sides that have vested interests in ensuring that the relationship stays on track.

Additionally, as the respected expert on U.S.-India relations Dr. Ashley Tellis has pointed out, the United States will need to find ways to engage India and enhance its infrastructure and military capabilities without a guaranteed quid pro quo. Such a transactional relationship raises serious political hackles in New Delhi, and Washington would better off seeing such efforts as investments in a long-term relationship rather than as concessions requiring an equal and reciprocal concession. Indeed, one could argue that a more capable India is fundamentally in American interests, in that it will enable New Delhi to more effectively contribute to regional stability while also complicating military planning for Beijing. For its part, as Dr. Tellis argues, India will need to keep Washington's attention by demonstrating its utility and reliability as a strategic partner without devolving the relationship into transactionalism. This will mean regular engagement, articulating a worldview that supports a special role for the United States in the world, as well as concrete examples of help and support on issues of interest and importance for the United States.

Over time, the potential for U.S.-India relations is tremendous. As a major rising power and a democracy with a very beneficial strategic geography, India has the potential to be a very important partner for the United States. Conversely, America's many financial and technological attributes, as well as its democratic politics and its respect for national autonomy, make the United States an attractive partner for New Delhi. The challenge for leaders on both sides will be overcoming the serious differences in worldview that remain, and translating potential into reality.

SUSTAINING AMERICAN POWER AND INFLUENCE

Some argue that the emerging distribution of power is one of American decline in the face of a rising China. While it is true that other countries have economies that are rising more quickly than ours, and that China's economy may have already eclipsed the American economy in overall GDP, I strongly disagree with the assessment that the United States is in decline. If anything, we are on the rise and will remain the most powerful nation in the world for the foreseeable future. Our economy is the most robust, innovative, and resilient in the world. The energy revolution that the United States has experienced in recent years is revolutionizing the geopolitics of the energy market, and providing the United States with new economic and geopolitical opportunities that no other country has the option to pursue. Despite ongoing problems and intensifying partisanship in our politics, the U.S. government and political system are fundamentally stable. We enjoy a global network of alliances and partnerships that is entirely unique and unrivaled in the world, and which enables our global political influence and military access. Our military might is unmatched in both its reach and capability. Our demographics are robust and suggest that the United States will not fall prey to the emerging population challenges that many countries around the world are just beginning to recognize. Finally, the United States has long benefited from a resilient international order based on robust rules and institutions. All of these advantages ensure that the foundations of American power will remain strong for the foreseeable future.

Yet despite the fact that the United States is likely to remain the dominant power in Asia for years to come, the power dynamics in the region are increasingly complex, as new and more established powers cooperate and compete in the advancement of their own interests. The continued power and influence of the United States will not come automatically. Indeed, while the United States has what it takes to remain dominant, doing so will require Washington to provide the necessary investments, resources, engagement, and strategies to sustain our power and influence in the world's most vital region. This is the vital role that Congress has to play. America will not long remain the most powerful nation in the Asia-Pacific if we do not do what it takes to sustain our geopolitical advantages.

I look forward to discussing the major geopolitical trends and dynamics affecting the Asia-Pacific, and how the United States can best position itself to sustain its power and leadership in the region. I look forward to your questions, and I would again like to extend my thanks and appreciation for inviting me to testify before you today.

———————

Mr. SALMON. Thank you. Mr. Mulloy.

STATEMENT OF THE HONORABLE PATRICK MULLOY, TRADE LAWYER (FORMER COMMISSIONER, U.S.-CHINA ECONOMIC AND SECURITY COMMISSION)

Mr. MULLOY. Mr. Chairman, Ranking Member Sherman, and members of the subcommittee, thank you for inviting me to testify about U.S. opportunities and challenges in the Asia-Pacific area.

I had the great good fortune in my life to work 15 years on the staff of the U.S. Senate Banking Committee where I was General Counsel and Chief International Counsel, so I love working with the elected representatives of people. And I think some of my views about what's happening in Asia may be reflective of the fact that I did have the chance to work for people who have to get elected to office.

I have already submitted my written testimony to the subcommittee, and I just want to take a little time here to hit some of the key points that I made in my written testimony.

I think America's so called pivot to Asia and a TPP as one element of the pivot are grounded in concerns about the rapid rise of China's economic, political, and military power. The pivot includes, among other things, beefing up our military capabilities, and building a closer working relationship with Japan and India.

I understand that by 2020, the Navy and Air Force plan to base 60 percent of their forces in the Asia-Pacific region. The pivot also makes a more vigorous attempt to integrate our economic relationship with Asian economies, such as those with whom we are negotiating the TPP.

I should note that we presently have a combined total trade deficit with the TPP countries of well over $100 billion. I hear a lot about the geopolitical reasons we must do the TPP, but I am not aware of any analysis that claims the TPP deal, if approved, would reduce our very large trade deficits with the TPP countries.

I also hear a lot about how the TPP, whose provisions I have not seen, will bring about increased exports from the U.S., but I hear nothing, nothing about what we might expect in terms of increased imports. Most economists will tell you that when a nation runs large negative net exports, you are detracting from your GDP and job growth.

The Chinese use a term called comprehensive national power, meaning that if you build your economy, then your military and political strength will come from that economic base.

Our completely unbalanced trade and economic policies toward China are helping China to become a great power much more quickly than we ever thought imaginable. Let me explain. I think we must correct our totally unbalanced economic relationship with China if we want to strengthen America's geopolitical position in Asia, and elsewhere.

Last year, our nation ran a $345 billion trade deficit with China. Since China joined the WTO in 2001, we have run over $3 trillion worth of trade deficits with China. How has China done this? One, they manipulated their currency. Two, they're stealing intellectual property. Three, they're incentivizing American companies to transfer factories from here to there partially through their currency manipulation. The companies can make bigger profits by moving there and shipping back here. China also incentivizes our companies to transfer technology and R&D from here to China. This is building China's military and industrial base. And then some people say then we have to arm ourselves because China is more powerful. I'm like the Congressman. I'm a trade hawk, and I'm not so keen on just using military means to rebalance this whole relationship.

I had the great good fortune, as well, to be a Commissioner on the U.S.-China Economic and Security Review Commission. That is a bipartisan group appointed by the leaders of the House and the Senate, and they're charged to look at the economic—at the national security implications of our economic relationship with China.

Most of their reports have been unanimous. In their 2014 report to the Congress, which is unanimous, the Commission said this:

> "China's rapid economic growth has enabled it to provide consistent and sizable increases to the PLA budget to support its military modernization. China's defense budget has increased by double digits every year since 1989."

Let me just finish this last part. They said,

> "As a result of China's comprehensive and rapid military modernization, the regional balance of power between China on the one hand, and the U.S. and its associates and allies on the other is shifting in China's direction."

So, it is clear that our imbalanced trade with China, that has fed China's extraordinary economic growth—over 10 percent a year for over 30 years—is contributing to a shift in the balance of power in Asia against our interests.

To me, we've got to pay a lot of attention to rebalancing this whole economic relationship with China. I have provided some ideas on how we might do that in my written testimony.

Thank you for giving me the opportunity to testify, and I look forward to taking any questions you may have.

[The prepared statement of Mr. Mulloy follows:]

Testimony of Patrick A. Mulloy
Trade Lawyer
Before the House Committee on Foreign Affairs
Subcommittee on Asia and the Pacific
Hearing Entitled
"Across the Pond: U.S. Opportunities and
Challenges in the Asia Pacific"
February 26, 2015

Chairman Salmon, Ranking Member Sherman, and Members of the Subcommittee, thank you for providing me with this opportunity to speak to you today on "U.S. Opportunities and Challenges in the Asia Pacific."

I commend the Subcommittee for holding this important hearing and am honored by the invitation to testify. I take great pride in, and it is a source of enormous personal satisfaction, to have served in a bipartisan manner on the staff of the Senate Banking Committee from 1983 to 1998. I very much enjoyed working for the elected representatives of the people. I also enjoyed my ten years of service as a Commissioner on the bipartisan and bicameral U.S.-China Economic and Security Review Commission. Seven of the Commission Reports to Congress during my tenure were adopted unanimously by all 12 Commissioners. Two others were adopted by votes of 11 to 1. On those two, I was with the 11. The Commission, some of whose views I will refer to in my testimony, is charged by the Congress "to monitor, investigate and report to the Congress on the national security implications of the bilateral trade and economic relationship between the United States and the People's Republic of China." That trade and economic relationship, which is completely out of balance and damaging to our nation, will be the focus of my testimony here today. I think the Commission, which Congress created, is a valuable asset to the Congress and the American people. It is the only think tank I know of which is integrating our economic and trade relationship with China with the military and geopolitical aspects as well.

China's Rise and the Pivot to Asia and the TPP as Responses

I think America's so-called "pivot" to Asia and the Trans Pacific Partnership Trade Agreement (TPP), as part of that pivot, are both grounded on concerns about the rapid rise of China's economic, political and military power. The pivot includes, among other things, beefing up our military capabilities in Asia and building a closer military working relationship with

Japan and India. I understand that by 2020 the navy and air force plan to base 60 percent of their forces in the Asia Pacific region. It also involves a more vigorous presence in Asian centered groups such as APEC, increased attention to the ASEAN nations, and a more integrated economic relationship with Asian economies such as those with whom we are negotiating the TPP.

I should note that we presently have a combined total trade deficit with the TPP countries, with whom we are negotiating, of over $100 billion. I am now hearing a lot about the geopolitical reasons we must do the TPP, but I am not aware of any analysis that claims the TPP deal, if approved, would reduce our very large trade deficit with the TPP countries. I also hear a lot of talk about how the TPP, whose provisions I have not seen, will bring about increased exports from the U.S. but nothing about what we might expect in terms of increased imports into the United States. At a minimum, we must ensure that we get provisions to address exchange rate manipulation into the TPP if we are to minimize what I expect will be a further detrimental impact on our job base and economy.

I believe, however, that the pivot to Asia will not succeed in its purpose as it does not adequately address the issues relative to China's growing economic strength upon which its increased military and political power is based. The Chinese use a term called "Comprehensive National Power" to describe the concept that if you build your economic power, it will be the basis upon which you will grow your political and military strength. Our trade and economic policies toward China, which are totally out of balance, are helping them to achieve their goal of being a Great Power much sooner than most had thought imaginable ten years ago. Instead of addressing that imbalance problem head on, we are in our pivot and TPP initiatives talking around it. We even talk about bringing China into the TPP later. Let me explain why I think we must correct our totally imbalanced economic relationship with China if we want to strengthen America's geopolitical position in Asia and elsewhere. .

What Drives China

China was for thousands of years the dominant power and civilization in Asia as well as the world's wealthiest society. The Chinese considered their Emperor, the supreme political authority, and themselves the geopolitical center of the world. Henry Kissinger has told us that "as late as1820 China produced over 30% of the world's GDP, an amount exceeding the GDP of Western Europe, Eastern Europe, and the United States combined."

Beginning with the First Opium War, in 1843, in which the British defeated Chinese efforts to stop the importation of opium by British companies, China fell rapidly from its high perch and suffered economic collapse and partial dismemberment in what its leaders refer to as a "Century of Humiliation." This ended in 1949 when Mao Tse Tung united China under one government controlled by the Communist Party. During the over 100 years of China's decline, the noted China scholar David Lampton has told us that the universal goal of China's people was to "make China rich and powerful and to regain the nation's former status as a great power that controls its own fate."

From 1949 to his death in 1976, Mao and his Communist-controlled government attempted, without success, to restore China's great power status by rebuilding its economy through a domestic-based and centrally-planned autarkic economy. They failed. At the time of Mao's death in September 1976 the country was still mired in poverty. Its total population of 900 million people produced a GDP of only $200 billion.

In 1978 Deng Xiaoping, emerged as China's new ruler. Deng knew Mao's economic policies had failed, and wanted to find a different way for China to rebuild its economic strength in order to provide a base for building its military and political power. Deng decided China needed foreign investment, foreign technology, foreign know-how and foreign markets to grow its economy and power. As a first step in that strategy he focused on obtaining formal recognition from the United States that his Communist Party was the legitimate government of China and to obtain "Most Favored Nation (MFN)" trade status from the United States. He got both in 1979. This enabled China to begin its export led growth strategy.

Prior to 1979, and the granting of MFN tariff treatment by the United States, Chinese goods coming to the U.S. would have faced an average tariff of over 40%. Once China got MFN trade treatment, that average tariff was reduced to around 4%. China, under Deng's leadership, then used various subsidies and strategies, including tax forgiveness, free land, cheap labor, and lax environmental laws to encourage American and other foreign companies to make greater profits by moving production to China and exporting to the U.S. and other markets outside of China. Foreign companies were also persuaded to transfer know-how and technology to China through joint venture investment agreements. China also sent its students abroad to get good educations in math, engineering and the sciences,

China also began a practice of underpricing its currency to give Chinese produced goods a further export subsidy, and to make it more difficult for American companies to export to China. When our dollar is overpriced, American companies are incentivized to invest in China to service Chinese customers not export from here to there. China also adopted a "value added tax" policy that rebates the tax on Chinese-produced goods made for export. In 1980 the U.S. trade deficit with China was $500 million. In 2000 it was over $83 billion. In 1980 China's GDP was $400 billion. In 2014, according to the IMF's *World Economic Outlook*, China's GDP was $17.63 billion, larger than America's $17.42 trillion. So China's export-led growth strategy has been an enormous success in building China's economic strength but has had a very detrimental impact of our job base and economy.

Another key step to encouraging Western investment into China was that nation's entry into the WTO in 2001. Prior to China's entering into the WTO, the U.S. gave China MFN trade treatment only one year at a time, and we had the ability to revoke it. China's government believed that if the U.S. market was locked open by a grant of permanent MFN, which WTO participants had to grant each other, it would increase foreign investment into China. It would bring about more exports by foreign companies to their home markets. It worked. In joining the WTO China also wanted to nullify the ability of the U.S. to unilaterally use Section 301 of its trade law to sanction China for unfair trade practices, such as currency manipulation and the theft of intellectual property. Under WTO procedures such sanctions could only be done by first winning a case in WTO dispute settlement, which is a lengthy and altogether unsatisfactory process. This took away leverage from the U.S. to ensure that China would not engage in these unfair trade practices.

After China joined the WTO in December 2001 new foreign investment poured into China as American and other foreign companies moved more of their manufacturing capabilities there. Our annual trade deficit with China grew from $83 billion in 2000 to over $340 billion in 2014. Of that $340 billion, our trade deficit with China in advanced technology products was over $123 billion.

Transfers of Technology and R & D

Although China pledged in its WTO entry commitment not to force U.S. companies to transfer technology for market access, as it was doing prior to 2001, China is now using its market to leverage technology out of foreign firms on the basis that they are doing so voluntarily and not by force. The companies are making decisions to transfer sophisticated technology and R& D activities to China in order to be considered "friends of China" with a hope to receive better treatment for their operations in China. If one U.S. company does this, it may not have a great impact, but when it becomes a general practice it can harm America's ability to innovate and compete. These technology transfers and R&D operations are also helping China to move up the technology chain and to improve its defense industrial base and its military capabilities.

Intellectual Property (IP) Theft

The Chinese also move up the technology chain by the theft of intellectual property. Jon Huntsman, a former Governor and former Ambassador to China last year co-authored a report on China's theft of intellectual property in violation of its WTO commitments. That Report stated:

> National industrial policy goals in China encourage IP theft and an
> extraordinary number of Chinese business and government officials
> are engaged in this practice.

Again the theft of intellectual property by China is costing the United States billions of dollars in profits to our companies and hundreds of thousands of good paying jobs for our citizens. It also aids China's efforts to move up the technology chain.

Currency Manipulation by China

The China Commission, on which I served, in its very first report to the Congress in July of 2002 noted that China was making large official purchases of U.S. dollars to maintain an underpriced currency. The Commission noted that by holding down the price of its currency, China was gaining an unfair trade advantage that was increasing our trade deficit with China. China has continued this practice for over a dozen years in complete violation of both its WTO and IMF treaty obligations.

Article XV of the WTO entitled "Exchange Arrangements" states in part that "Contracting parties shall not by exchange actions frustrate the intent of the provisions of this Agreement, nor by trade actions the provisions of the Articles of Agreement of the International Monetary Fund." The intent of the GATT/WTO Agreement as spelled out in its preamble was "reciprocal and mutually advantageous arrangements related to the substantial reduction of tariffs and other barriers to trade and to the elimination of discriminatory treatment in international commerce."

Article I of the IMF Charter, to which China belongs, states that one of its purposes is to "promote exchange stability, to maintain orderly exchange arrangements among members, and to avoid competitive exchange depreciations." Article IV of the IMF Charter entitled "Obligations Regarding Exchange Arrangements" obligates each member nation from manipulating its currency "to gain an unfair competitive advantage over other members."

The IMF has adopted surveillance provisions to guide its members on how this Article IV should be interpreted. It indicated currency manipulation under the Article could be defined as "protracted large scale intervention in the exchange market" and the "excessive accumulation of foreign currency reserves." Moreover there is a direct linkage between WTO/GATT Article XV and IMF Article IV since Article XV states that the WTO when dealing with problems regarding exchange practices shall consult fully with the IMF

China has for years been blatantly violating both its IMF and WTO exchange rate obligations by intervening in currency markets to purchase trillions of dollars in order to prop up the dollar's value against the yuan. China has run over \$3 trillion in trade surpluses with the United States just since 2001 and has invested these dollars in U.S. Treasuries and other U. S. debt obligations as part of the manner by which it underprices its currency. China now has almost \$4 trillion dollars in foreign currency reserves. This amount is larger than the GDP's of India, South Korea and Thailand combined and gives China the ability to advance its interests in Asia, Africa and South America. Groups of Americans injured by China's currency practices petitioned USTR to bring a WTO case against China under Article XV but that agency refused to do so.

Pressure on U.S. Companies to Lobby Congress

One of America's most influential China experts is Dr. Kenneth Lieberthal, who as the former senior director for China on the National Security Council, strongly favored bringing

China into the WTO in 2001. Nevertheless he noted on page 89 of his 2011 book entitled *Managing the China Challenge* that:

> When Congress debates trade distorting legislation that targets China,
> it is not unusual for the Chinese Government through its Embassy
> in Washington or other channels, to pressure multinational
> corporations to weigh in to prevent the legislation from passing.

This could help explain why the multinational corporations have not supported legislation passed by both Houses of Congress, in different years. That legislation would have enabled domestic companies, injured by imports from China that are subsidized by an underpriced currency, to bring countervailing duty cases against the importers.

China's Growing Economy Feeds Its Military Spending

The U.S. China Economic and Security Review Commission in its 2014 Report to the Congress stated:

> China's rapid economic growth has enabled it to provide
> consistent and sizeable increases to the PLA budget to
> support its military modernization…China's defense
> budget has increased by double digits every year since 1989.

It indicated that China's growing confidence in its military capabilities underpins its aggressive behavior in the East and South China Seas since 2009. The Commission also stated unanimously in its 2014 Report:

> As a result of China's comprehensive and rapid military
> modernization, the regional balance of power between China,
> on the one hand, and the U.S. and its allies and associates on
> the other, is shifting in China's direction.

So it is clear that our imbalanced trade with China, that helps feed China's extraordinary economic growth, is contributing to a shift in the balance of power in Asia against our interests.

Impact of Our China Trade Imbalance on the U.S.

The many ways that China has used to grow its economy and enrich a portion of its populace has also caused major problems in the U.S. economy. These problems include the theft of intellectual property that harms innovation here and the outsourcing of production by U.S. manufacturers to China that also hurts America's ability to innovate and even make items essential to our defense capabilities. Business experts have pointed out that when we outsource so much of our industrial production, we are weakening out industrial commons and our ability to innovate new products. The outsourcing of production also results in a loss of tax revenues for our nation, states, and communities, increases unemployment, and contributes to our massive trade deficits which feed our exploding international debt problem. The latter will lead to increasing ownership of the U.S. economy by Chinese state owned enterprises. Let me explain that point.

Warren Buffett, in a famous article that appeared in *Fortune Magazine* on October 23, 2003, told us that the trade deficit was selling the country out from under us. He noted when we run a trade deficit it means we are living better than we are earning. He likened our nation to a rich family that possesses a large farm, but that is no longer earning its way, and thus has to sell off a part of the farm each year. He said it was imperative that we take "action to halt he outflow of our national wealth."

The Chinese now have enormous amounts of money to buy assets in this county. According to the China Commission unlike their investments in developing countries, where they are buying natural resources, the Chinese are focusing on buying famous brands and manufacturing technologies in this country. Some years ago Dr. Alan Bromley, the first President Bush's science advisor warned policymakers that "our technology base can be nibbled from under us through a coherent plan of purchasing entrepreneurial companies." We need to make sure we have an adequate CFIUS policy in place to review the increasing purchases of U.S. companies by Chinese investors. It is important to know that outbound investment from China needs government approval and Chinese companies, even non-state owned ones, can receive government funding to finance their purchases here. Increased Chinese foreign investment here, which is the other side of our trade deficit with China, will also give China more political influence in our open democracy.

What is to be Done: Immediate Trade And Investment Steps?

America's political leaders must realize that the United States has thrown its citizens into an increasingly competitive global economy in which many of our Asian trading partners such as China, Korea, Japan and Taiwan have national goals and strategies to move their economies forward. Underpricing their currencies to achieve trade surpluses and attract investment is just one part of such strategies. We must develop our own strategy to compete in such a world. Among the points in such a strategy must be measures to aggressively address mercantilist trade practices, being used by China and some our other key Asian trading partners to achieve trade surpluses with us. These practices include currency manipulation, barriers to imports, illegal export subsidies, forced technology transfers, and the massive theft of intellectual property. Included in our strategy or "business plan" if you will, should be:

1. Treating goods imported here from countries that are underpricing their currencies as subsidized imports to which increased duties can be applied under our unfair trade laws.

2. Bringing a WTO case against China for manipulating its currency contrary to its obligations under Article XV.

3. Working within the IMF, to whom the WTO will turn for advice, to make sure its members join with us to have the IMF be more aggressive in policing violations of its Article IV prohibition against currency manipulation.

4. Strengthening our CFIUS review of foreign investment coming into the U.S. to make sure we are not permitting the acquisition of technologies important to our national security.

5. Granting companies an antitrust exception ,for coordinating trade strategies with other companies, against a country that is trying to extort concessions from them.

6. Including penalties or snap back clauses in trade agreements that can be invoked against violators of such agreements.

What Is To Be Done: Setting Goals And Adopting Measures To Achieve Them

1) Set a National Goal to balance our trade account by a date certain, say 2025. Our massive trade deficits with Asian countries and others over the last ten years have cost us millions of manufacturing jobs and the loss of more than 60,000 factories. Our citizens are rightfully dubious about the merits of new free trade initiatives that are advanced by the same interests and groups who told us China's entry into the WTO would help balance our trade with China. If we have a balanced trade goal we can evaluate whether new trade initiatives will advance us toward such a goal.

2) Convene an Emergency National Summit on the trade deficit that would be attended by the President, relevant Cabinet Officers, bipartisan leadership of both Houses of Congress, and a small number of top corporate and labor leaders. Establish a BRAC type commission to develop some initial ideas on measures needed to balance trade and then have Congress, through multi-Committee hearings, develop a new trade bill as was done in 1988 when Congress developed and passed the Omnibus Trade and Competiveness Act.

3) Align corporate and national interests: Other countries have instituted practices that give incentives to U.S. and multinational corporations to help them grow their own economies at our expense. Our corporations are operating in a system that compels them to focus on making profits for their shareholders. Top corporate officials get significant financial rewards for achieving these objectives. Our nation must develop policies to counter foreign practices designed to entice our corporations to serve their interests. We must find the means to align the interests of American based corporations with the national interest ,which includes keeping and creating well paying high tech jobs in this country and not transferring huge chunks of our productive capabilities out of the country. One such incentive might be to reduce corporate taxes on corporations that add to U.S. jobs and GDP by producing in this country, and to put higher taxes on corporations that earn their profits by producing abroad and shipping back here.

Thank you again for inviting me to present my views on these important matters. I will pleased to answer any questions that you may have for me.

68

Mr. SALMON. Thank you. That concludes the panel testimonies. We'd like to now be able to ask some questions.

First of all, regarding these maritime disputes both in the South China and East China Seas, and in light of this month's reports that China is building artificial islands, and potentially building up military installations, what is the administration's response? And do you see it as effective? Start with you, Dr. Jackson, what are your thoughts?

Mr. VAN JACKSON. Yes.

Mr. SALMON. Yes. Okay, thank you.

Mr. VAN JACKSON. Thank you. So, the administration has taken steps to shore up its alliances. It's focused—it's taken its own credibility in the region seriously. The challenge is not so much with the United States sort of showing up, or demonstrating resolve short of violence, or the threat of great violence. The larger issue is with the nuanced way that China is doing what it's doing.

It makes it much easier to stand firm or retaliate whenever the Chinese send in the PLA Navy. Right? Whenever they use traditional military force it's easy to respond in kind. Signaling resolve in this kind of thing becomes a clearer exercise, but when you're using unarmed drones, when you're pressing assertive with the construction of artificial islands or water canons, or any of these sort of nontraditional means, it creates this dynamic where it's very hard to respond without being seen as the bad guy, without being seen as escalatory yourself.

I think there's a way to remedy this by sort of forcing operational transparency to the extent possible through cooperation, information sharing regimes with allies and partners. It's something that China can be a part of, too, if it wanted to. The question is does it want to? And as long as China operates coercion within this gray space, transparency is really the only solution without sort of risking escalation, I think.

Mr. SALMON. Thank you. Yes, Dr. Jackson.

Mr. KARL JACKSON. I would just say that, to amplify the answer of my fellow Jackson member here, that China really follows, if you look at it in a long term, a take and then talk strategy. It's cyclical. The number of incidents go up in the South China Sea, or in the East China Sea, and then if there's an APEC meeting coming in Beijing, suddenly things get quiet in the Pacific again. And then I would assume we're moving into—in fact, we're in the middle of the next phase of a take strategy, which is the creation of new islands in the South China Sea. And, you know, this is a very difficult problem to deal with, and it requires, in my opinion, that the administration provide more assistance to the Philippines, more diplomatic assistance, as well as military assistance. Thank you.

Mr. SALMON. Thank you. Over the last few years, the tensions in the Taiwan Strait have de-escalated with the election of President Ma. He's facing some political challenges of his own, and recently there's speculation that the DPP candidate may gain a little bit of steam given some of his challenges.

China has made no secret of its loathing of the DPP and what they stand for. If the DPP is successful in the next election, where do you see Taiwan-China-U.S. relations going? Any thoughts? Mr. Denmark, did you want to address that?

Mr. DENMARK. Sure. Obviously, we're still quite a ways away from the next Taiwan Presidential election, so it's difficult to speculate on who may win. But I do think that the Mainland is being very careful to try to keep some space open in case a DPP candidate wins so that they'd be able to maintain a relationship with Taiwan.

They, obviously, recognize that it's very—it's going to be very complicated if the DPP wins the next Presidential election in Taiwan. There's going to be a lot of concern in China that the next candidate would show some of the more problematic tendencies that Chen Shui-bian showed when the DPP was last in power. But I also think that the Mainland would be trying to find a space that they can work with the DPP, so I expect them to be fairly quiet about the election. I'm not trying to put anybody in a corner, but I do think that they're going to be very concerned about what happens.

I also wanted to note that there's going to be some real challenges in the next election, and if—whoever wins the next election in Taiwan, because of what's happened last year in Hong Kong, because of the framework that China talks about these systems of one country, two systems; although, the proposals are not exactly the same. There are some important differences, but they are some very important similarities, as well; enough similarities that I think in Taiwan there will be a lot of concerns and questions about this formulation of one country, two systems, and how Taiwan can position itself within that context.

Mr. SALMON. I completely concur. In fact, I think the Taiwan body has been really watching with interest how this whole one country, two systems has played out. And it hasn't really played out the way that China said it would back in 1997. They have not been nearly as hands off, especially with the selection of the CEO, as they said they would be. And it's prompted these protests and quite a bit of political unrest within Hong Kong. And I don't think that is helping their case at all with Taiwan as they seek a peaceful reunification at some point in the future. I think it bodes very ill for them.

In fact, I'm going to be leading a codel in May with Elliot Engel to Hong Kong, specifically, for these purposes, so stay tuned. I'll yield to Mr. Bera.

Mr. BERA. I want to thank my colleague from California for giving me this time.

It is a very interesting time in this pivot to Asia, and as we look at the U.S.-Asia relationship, as we look at the opportunities and the challenges, listening to the opening testimony, the goal is twofold; stability in the region and prosperity in the region. And, certainly, that is to our advantage.

Having had the privilege to travel to India with the President and, you know, just kind of up front looking at the dual interests on both sides; clearly, I think at the Executive level the Prime Minister and the President understand the importance of the relationship. I think the Prime Minister as he is looking at an ambitious agenda in India, is looking for reliable partners, and clearly is looking to the West. Certainly, is building a relationship with Japan, but also increasingly is looking at the importance of the relation-

ship with the United States. And I think the President understands the opportunities to open up the Indian markets here. And
then, also, the importance of India geopolitically and strategically
in stabilizing South Asia, and helping bring some stability to the
South China Sea and so forth.

I think we make a mistake if we just look at these relationships
in a bilateral way, though, because there are really trilateral, multilateral relationships. And when we think about the U.S.-India relationship, we should also think about the U.S.-India-Japan relationship because, again, it's in our interests as allies. Certainly,
India is looking at these relationships in a multilateral way. I
think we make a mistake if we just look at India as picking the
United States or China. Again, all these countries have major trading relationships with China, as well; and, again, I think we approach these in a multilateral relationship.

You know, I'd be curious, you know, as we look at this growing
relationship with India, as we've set the framework in moving forward with another 10-year bilateral defense treaty, looking forward
to continuing progress on a bilateral investment treaty with India,
and so forth, there's real opportunities here in the U.S.-India space
to protect our interests but also, again, to bring stability to the region. Maybe we'll start with Mr. Denmark, your thoughts on this.

Mr. DENMARK. Thank you, Congressman.

I completely agree with the tremendous potential there is in the
U.S.-India relationship. I actually happened to be in New Delhi
when Xi Jinping was visiting and got to see what a problematic relationship that India has with China.

Clearly, Prime Minister Modi is seeking to enhance his relationships with all the major countries in Asia, so he's had important
visits with President Obama, with Xi Jinping, but also with Putin,
with Abe, and with Abbott down in Australia. But I think, clearly,
that the United States occupies a special place in Prime Minister's
Modi's outlook. And the bilateral defense agreement, the investment agreement that you mentioned I think have tremendous potential both in themselves, and what we can work with them, but
also the precedents that they set; that the bilateral agreements
that we've already put together with India, the Ash Carter push
when he was the deputy, now his secretary, I think have tremendous potential to enhance our defense technology cooperation capabilities, potentially our interoperability, our planning. And because
we share so many interests, especially in East Asia with India. On
the investment side, encouraging India to look more outward as an
exporter, to be a more integrated member of the international economy, I think is of vital importance.

And I would just add, finally, you mentioned the trilateral and
quadrilateral agreements, aspects of this relationship. Prime Minister Modi had very interesting and very close engagements with
Prime Minister Abe, and with Abbott in Australia, and I think
there's real potential for that quadrilateral dynamic that I hope in
the coming years we'll see really getting——

Mr. BERA. Great. And I'm glad you mentioned the new Secretary
of Defense, Ash Carter. I think we've got a great team in place that
understands the complexity of the region, as well as the opportunity. Obviously, the Secretary of Defense understands the region

and spent a lot of time there. Our new Ambassador to India, Rich Verma, certainly understands the complexity and the opportunities there, as well.

Mr. Goodman, you talked about kind of a basis of economic stability and economic prosperity. In the extreme seconds that I have left, would you like to go ahead and expand on that?

Mr. GOODMAN. Sure. Again, the same basic point, which is there's huge potential in the U.S.-India relationship in the economic front. It's been, frankly, under-exploited over a long period of time. I think that that's for a number of reasons. I think one of them is that India has not until Prime Minister Modi in recent times had somewhat committed to the internal economic reform that Modi seems to be clearly committed to. And I think that's a precondition to a stronger relationship.

Then there are the direct bilateral processes you mentioned. The bilateral investment treaty I think has great potential. I think it's going to be a challenging negotiation, but I do think it's something that could provide a real foundation.

There are number of outstanding concerns, particularly of our U.S. businesses in India with foreign investment restrictions, localization requirements, intellectual property problems, the patent protection and so forth. Modi has addressed some of those. There's been some improvement on foreign direct investment in the railways and other infrastructure sectors, and I think that's quite an important sort of down payment on an improvement.

I also would just endorse the point that regionally there's a big opportunity. You know, frankly, India has not been as engaged in certainly regional economic affairs to the extent that I think would be good for all of us. And they're not a member of APEC, which is the fault of both sides really for their not being in there. But they've also been sort of lukewarm about some of these regional endeavors. And I actually think that there would be, if they were willing to invest in a more greater openness in their own economy, they could make a great contribution to rulemaking and principle in these regional arrangements.

Mr. BERA. Great, and I would just close with this. As co-chair of the Caucus on India and Indian-Americans which is the largest country caucus in Congress, I think I can speak for members on both sides of the aisle that we view the U.S.-India relationship in a bilateral way, and see some of the opportunities there. Thank you.

Mr. SALMON. Great. Thank you. Mr. Rohrabacher.

Mr. ROHRABACHER. First and foremost, thank you, Mr. Chairman for holding this hearing, and with these five very informative witnesses.

Dr. Mulloy, or Mr. Mulloy mentioned that in the TPP he did not see anything that was going to bring down the level of trade deficit with the Pacific, which is now $100 billion a year, and with China it is $350 billion a year trade deficit. Do any of you disagree with Mr. Mulloy's assessment that there's nothing in the TPP that will bring that down? Are you predicting that the trade deficit will go down if we pass this trade policy? Yes, whoever. Does anyone disagree with him on that?

Mr. GOODMAN. Well, I think it's very unclear how bilateral trade deficits and surpluses will be affected by trade agreements like this. I think in principle, a trade agreement like TPP which is opening markets in some of these key markets in Asia will increase our export opportunities. Of the 23 trade agreements that we've negotiated since 2000, all but one of them has led to a significant increase in U.S. exports. The one that hasn't is the Korea free trade agreement, and that's largely because Korea hasn't been growing and, therefore, particularly our coal exports to Korea have really plummeted. Our corn exports have also plummeted because of drought here. But if you take out those factors, other exports to Korea have increased. There should be an expectation of greater trade and exports to those countries.

I would like to take on one point——

Mr. ROHRABACHER. Before you do.

Mr. GOODMAN. Yes?

Mr. ROHRABACHER. Do you actually know what's in the TPP, because——

Mr. GOODMAN. I mean, I haven't read the actual agreement itself, but I have a general sense of what the contents are, yes.

Mr. ROHRABACHER. Because we're not even permitted to know exactly what it's in the TPP. I mean, I've got people telling us what it's about. It's interesting they can read it and we can't. What's going on here?

You were about to make a point. I'm sorry for cutting you off.

Mr. GOODMAN. No, no, it's all right.

Mr. ROHRABACHER. I'd like Mr. Mulloy to have his chance to answer you, but go ahead.

Mr. GOODMAN. Sure. No, I have not read the TPP agreement, so I am basing my understanding or assessment of it on the presentation by the U.S. Trade Representative Office, and by other players in TPP, what the contents are.

Mr. ROHRABACHER. Have they been successful. You're basing it on them; have they been successful in their predictions in the past?

Mr. GOODMAN. Well, I mean, I think trade has increased with the countries with which we've negotiated free trade agreements, so I think in that sense yes.

Mr. ROHRABACHER. Okay.

Mr. GOODMAN. We'll see what TPP actually does.

I just wanted to respond to one thing about imports. So, I mean, this is a somewhat controversial statement to say, but imports are not as bad as people say in the sense that we're all working—I mean, it's like we work 5 days a week, that's exporting, to have the weekend, that's importing. We all want our iPhones. Right? We all want our, sorry, Smart Phones, which are made up of value from all around the world. You buy it for a couple of hundred dollars. When it arrives in Long Beach, it's valued at about $170, and that is booked by customs as an import from China worth $170. The reality is only about $6 worth of this phone is actually produced in China, the rest is value-added from all over the world, including the United States. So, I think our trade data is not entirely an accurate reflection of global value chain production today. That's the specific point I——

Mr. ROHRABACHER. Give Mr. Mulloy a chance to answer.

Ordinary working people who have jobs producing high-quality products in the United States has enabled us to have a very wealthy, not a wealthy, but a middle class who lives at a decent standard of living. I personally see that in jeopardy, and by basically people who make analysis all based on what's good for a business, which then translates sometimes just into very wealthy Americans are getting better, but middle class Americans are not because they don't have these high-quality jobs.

We've got just a couple of minutes, or a couple of seconds. Go right ahead.

Mr. MULLOY. Thank you, Congressman. I remember the debate about whether to give China PNTR and bring them into the WTO. Many of the same groups, which are now behind the TPP, talk about increasing exports. I remember those same people were telling us that if we brought China into the WTO—we had an $80 billion trade deficit with China at that time, now we have a $345 billion annual trade deficit with China. So, they told us that it would help balance our trade. It didn't, it made the situation much worse.

I remember being on the staff of the Senate Banking Committee when we did hearings on NAFTA, and we were being told that it would help expand and improve our trade relationship with Mexico. We have about a $70 billion trade deficit with Mexico now after that, because there were no currency provisions in that agreement. And shortly after it was signed, Mexico devalued their currency. And that was—when we looked at it, we saw that wasn't a trade agreement, that was an investment agreement. And that's why they wanted those investor state provisions in that agreement to protect their right not to have to settle disputes in Mexican courts. So, I hear a lot of talk about the TPP exports. I never hear anybody talk about the trade balance that we're going to get out of this TPP. And I think that's very important for members to think about, and the impact that's going to have on their constituents.

Mr. ROHRABACHER. Well, thank you for bringing that up, and thank you, Mr. Chairman.

Just a note; we were also told that with more trade with China, by bringing them into a close economic relationship with the United States, that we would have democratization. And I notice Mr. Denmark's remarks, he went through all the isms that are happening in China, but democratization wasn't one of them. And, in fact, I think what we see now is a regime in China that is politically just as oppressive that its ever been, and the theory that we were going to have more democracy by having this more open economic relationship, which they have manipulated, has not worked out. And what I call it is we were given the hug a Nazi, make a liberal theory, and it didn't work. They're no more liberal in China than they ever were. Thank you very much, Mr. Chair.

Mr. SALMON. Thank you, Mr. Rohrabacher. Mr. Lowenthal.

Mr. LOWENTHAL. Yes, I find the conversations fascinating. I think that there's been a focus more—again, I'm going to bring it back to some of the—what's important to me is some of the smaller countries in Asia. We focused on China, and we focused on India. I've listened a lot. But I'm concerned about, as I mentioned in my opening statement, I talked about, and I'll give you some other examples. I'd really like to hear your thoughts.

I talked about some of the, what I consider—I represent Little Saigon, and Garden Grove, and Westminster, and all I hear from my constituents are the fact that human rights violations that are going on, and prisoners of conscience. And I also just recently introduced the International Human Rights Defense Act to protect—to create a special envoy within the Department of State for LGBT rights; and, yet, you know, I also—and as that bill was just beginning to be moved forward, Senator Markey also had the same bill, Secretary Kerry picked it up and appointed a special envoy for LGBT rights. Yet, we're talking about, just as Vietnam, we're talking about Brunei. Brunei puts LGBT folks to death, you know. It recently made same-sex sexual activity punishable by death; yet, it continues to be part of the TPP negotiations. We have some real issues of human rights violations also in Malaysia, in Singapore.

I'm wondering with this pivot is there a role that we can leverage, as I raised, on some of the smaller countries to—without imposing, but to really talk about, you know, you want to increase trade with the United States. What are you going to do about these issues, you know, that—and how are you going to really demonstrate beforehand that you're really moving forward at this time; or is that just not really a reasonable request to make at this time? You know, does that destabilize the situation?

We talked about needing—I think it was Mr. Jackson talked about—Dr. Jackson, about the need for stability. I mean, I'm more concerned about protection of human rights at this moment, so I'm just wondering. That would protect the stability within those nations.

Mr. KARL JACKSON. Well, you've posed a difficult question. I used to work a lot on human rights problems in Vietnam, and I used to interview people in Westminster.

Mr. LOWENTHAL. Right.

Mr. KARL JACKSON. I used to hang out with Dana Rohrabacher working on the same issues.

Mr. LOWENTHAL. And Dana has done a great job, and I now represent part of the—that Dana used to represent. So, I picked up the Dana Rohrabacher mantle; so, I'm following in the great tradition of Dana Rohrabacher.

Mr. KARL JACKSON. All of that said, the whole business of making foreign policies is prioritizing, making choices, tough choices. And while it is possible for us to try to the best of our ability via the State Department, the Defense Department, et cetera, to push Vietnam toward being more reasonable toward its citizens, we have not been very effective. It's been very difficult.

Mr. LOWENTHAL. Yet, now we're going to reward this bad behavior by having a special trade agreement.

Mr. KARL JACKSON. No, I think what we're going to do is reward ourselves by creating a more stable Asia-Pacific area by having this trade agreement. And, you know, nothing, nothing is going to come close to being perfect either with a trade agreement, or certainly with the human rights dimension. I've been doing this for a long time, and I wish I could say I've been 100% successful. It's not for lack of trying, but I don't think you're going to be able to turn to the Vietnamese administration and say all right, if you don't make the following six changes, there'll be no TPP. I think that would be a counterproductive way to go.

Mr. LOWENTHAL. For them, for us to say to them. What if I said to myself if you don't make those changes, I won't vote for it.

Mr. KARL JACKSON. That's your—you know, obviously——

Mr. LOWENTHAL. I'm just saying would that—do we have any leverage?

Mr. KARL JACKSON. We have only very limited leverage over what goes on at the domestic level inside Vietnam. I wish it were otherwise, Congressman.

Mr. MULLOY. Well, I think you have a lot of leverage because you haven't given TPA yet, and in the TPA you can say what you want addressed in these trade agreements, because if you're going to bring them back without having a chance to amend them, and you have to vote them up or down, you've got to be pretty clear what you want, and then follow-up and make sure that those items are on the agenda of the negotiators.

My problem now is, I think the TPP is being put to bed even before the TPA is going to be enacted, so you're going to come back without Congress really having a chance to put its input into this TPP in the way it should.

Mr. LOWENTHAL. I yield back.

Mr. SALMON. Thank you. Representative Meng.

Ms. MENG. Thank you to the witnesses for being here today.

My first question is for Dr. Van Jackson, or whoever, is welcome to answer, about North Korea. North Korea has been increasing its investment in nontraditional military weapons, chemical and cyber, in addition to its nuclear program. Is there any strategy that would dissuade North Korea from the further development of these weapons? I'm curious about your thoughts.

Mr. VAN JACKSON. So, the short answer is probably no, not in the near term, anyway. They've put nuclear weapons in their constitution so it's more than a bargaining chip at this point. It's increasingly becoming part of who they see themselves as being.

Chemical weapons, my interpretation has been that they see it not as a taboo the way we or the international community does, but as a sort of operational capability just like any other military capability. So, there's some reasonable expectation that chemical weapons could be used in some sort of limited conflict because they don't share the same taboo about it. But there is a larger pattern here where North Korean sort of egregious misdeeds, especially on the violence end, only occur in the context of sort of shared hostilities, which is very much the case right now, obviously. And we can— we and our South Korean ally can only bend so far, obviously, but it takes two to cooperate. It takes two to have, you know, a rapprochement, or non-hostile relations, qua amity from enmity. Right? So, all of the bad things we see from North Korea tend to be arrested during periods of better relations.

The question is, how can get there? And in the near term, I don't see a path, so it seems the responsible thing to do in that context then is to be prepared for the range of possibilities with North Korea.

Ms. MENG. My second question, anyone is welcome. the Asian-American diaspora is the fastest growing population in the United

States. How do you think this will impact our point of view and relationships with our allies in Asia?

Mr. KARL JACKSON. No, the increasing size of the Asian-American diaspora is a good thing. It's a very good thing, because of the fact it makes us much more informed about this place called Asia. And I think that anything that can be done to facilitate the movement of more Asian-Americans, for instance, into our diplomatic service would be a great plus.

We're beginning to see Korean Americans as Ambassadors and things like that. And, frankly, they receive a different reception in Asia. They are 100 percent American, but they have a different reception, and it's a very positive—it can be a very positive thing. Thank you.

Mr. MULLOY. Governor McAuliffe has recently appointed me to the Commonwealth's Asian Advisory Board in Virginia, so I'm having a great opportunity to meet a lot of very talented Asian Americans, and learn a lot. And I think they'll be a tremendous asset for this country going forward on giving this broader perspective on how we should be integrated with these Asian economies.

I'm a trade hawk, but I am very much in favor of balanced trade, and that's what I think we ought to be doing. I'm very much in favor of a closer economic relationship with India. I went to India when I was in the Clinton administration. I was Assistant Secretary, and before the President went out there, I was out there trying to line up some deliverables that the President could sign when he went out later. And I always thought that we should be putting a lot more attention on India. They're a democracy. Why are we putting all of our apples, and all of our effort into this China relationship? The imbalance in it I think is really harmful to this country, and I think we've got to rebalance that. But I think Asian Americans are going to be a tremendous asset to this country going forward.

Ms. MENG. Thank you. I yield back.

Mr. SALMON. Thank you. Mr. Connolly.

Mr. CONNOLLY. Have you gone, Brad? Entirely up to you, whatever you have scheduled. Thank you, sir.

Welcome to the panel and, Pat, great to see you again. Pat and I had the honor of serving together in the U.S. Senate as fellow staffers working with Senator Sarbanes, in particular; great preparation for this job, I'll tell you.

Pat, let me pick up on something you had to say about NAFTA. It sounded like what you were saying was Mexico deliberately waited until the ink was dry on the NAFTA agreement and then devalued its currency, thus, unfairly exploiting the opportunity NAFTA gave it. Is that your view of history?

Mr. MULLOY. No, here's my view. When we did the hearings in the Banking Committee on NAFTA, it was sold as a free trade agreement. But when you really held the hearings, you concluded that was really an investment agreement. It was to provide an opportunity for American companies to be able to invest more in Mexico, to have a lower base job—to have lower wages, and be able to compete with some of the Asian imports. That was kind of the theory of the thing. But we didn't have any currency provisions in that agreement. And the fact that you had those investor state provisions in it to get outside of the Mexican courts to protect American investors was a good sign it was an investment agreement. Senator Warren has a big article about that issue in The Washington Post today.

But shortly after that was done, Mexico ran into an economic emergency and devalued its currency, but we had no provisions in the NAFTA to deal with currency issues. I don't think they necessarily planned it, but it happened, and I think it had enormous deleterious impact on the American economy, and particularly those jobs in the Midwest where the companies relocated to Mexico and shipped back here.

Mr. CONNOLLY. Got it. Dr. Karl Jackson, sometimes in the world of political upheaval transformative change can happen virtually overnight. I mean, there may be lots of things that lead up to it, but the actual change happens very rapidly; witness the fall of the Berlin Wall, and everything that happened in Eastern Europe. I don't know any experts who predicted the rapidity of that change, and the reintegration of the two Germanies. I mean, nobody I knew at that time.

Are we prepared for something comparable in North Korea? What if change comes to North Korea, I mean, with lightning speed and the regime collapses, and now what do we do?

Mr. KARL JACKSON. Well, you've hit upon a really good problem, because of the fact that if there were really rapid uncontrolled regime change, this would make China extremely nervous. It would make South Korea extremely nervous, and it would make the United States extremely nervous. And this is an instance where if there were the kind of security arrangement that I was advocating in my written testimony, then the phones would ring in New Delhi, Washington, Tokyo, and Beijing, and we would hopefully all say to one another let's all be calm and take this one step at a time, no troop movements. Let us all try to let the situation sort itself out to the maximum degree possible. But it is a very worrisome thing, and Chinese officials worry about it just as much as you do, because uncontrolled change is the one thing they want to avoid. They don't want a flood of refugees, and more than anything else they don't want the kind of instability that might necessitate the south coming to the north.

Mr. CONNOLLY. Thank you. Mr. Denmark, I wish we had more time, but real quickly, Mr. Mulloy has given a pretty cogent critique of a potential TPP, but I wonder if you might address both that critique and—but what's the alternative? I mean, one of the things I wrestle with is, if we don't set the standards through TPP, and we let this fall, then by virtue of the vacuum, it seems to me the Chinese then set them. And that is part of the choice, I think, we're wrestling with up here.

Mr. DENMARK. Thank you, Mr. Chairman. And an aside, I'm very glad that you asked about Korean unification. I think it's an incredibly important issue.

On TPP, I am not an economist. I am not even going to—it's hard for a think tank person to admit his lack of expertise in something, but I'll admit I'm not an economist. I leave that to my friend, Mr. Goodman, here. But I can talk about the geopolitics of TPP; that TPP is absolutely essential to the longstanding American power

and influence in Asia; that economics is at the center of Asian geopolitics, and the United States needs to play a leading role in that
area; that TPP would go a long way in setting the rules of the road
for economic engagement in Asia that goes beyond the specifics of
the agreement, but would really set the tenor for much of economic
engagement across the Asia-Pacific. And if we don't set the rules
of the road, then China will. And if China is able to set the rules
of the road, as it is already attempting to do by establishing things
like the Asia Infrastructure Investment Bank and other sort of alternative institutions, we'll see much lower standards for environmental protection, lower standards for—lower tariffs for tariffs, and
just a lower quality mode of economic integration; something that
would be very much detrimental to our broader interest for greater
economic integration in the region. So, geopolitically I see the TPP
as being incredibly important.

Mr. CONNOLLY. I would only ask the chairman, Mr. Mulloy seeking recognition. It's the chairman's call, because my time is up.

Mr. SALMON. Mr. Sherman.

Mr. CONNOLLY. Thank you.

Mr. SHERMAN. There is an alternative. It's fair trade rather than
free trade. The question is not TPP, or the status quo. The question
is when we listened to Warren Buffet when he suggested that we
require that for every dollar of imports there be a dollar of exports.
The economic arguments for TPP are so bad that we have to be
told that somehow we're going to obtain a national security advantage. The benefit—China, actually, will be the beneficiary of TPP
because, as I indicated in my opening statement, goods could be ad-
mitted to be 65 percent made in China, but actually 70, 80, 90 percent made in China, and get duty-free access to the United States
under the "rules of origin." You just ship it to a TPP country, the
slap a Made in Vietnam sticker on it, and end it to the United
States, and we get no access to China.

And as to the joy of us writing the rules of the road, these are
Wall Street's rules. They have mutilated the American middle
class, and the fact that they were made in Wall Street doesn't
change that. The rules of the road in the future ought to be fair
trade.

But moving on to another subject, Mr. Jackson, and whichever
Mr. Jackson feels most focuses on this. Would China be less in-
clined to support the North Korean regime if they had a solid
promise from the United States that American forces will never be
deployed north of the DMZ, and that, in fact, a unified Korea would
have substantially fewer American forces in it than South Korea
does today?

Mr. VAN JACKSON. That's a good question. I don't think no matter what we promise that they would find it credible, ultimately.

Mr. SHERMAN. Even if it was a Senate-ratified treaty?

Mr. VAN JACKSON. Anything is possible, I suppose. I think the
reasonable hedge for China is to maintain a reasonably sized military garrison on the other side of its border, and as it has suggested, in the event of any kind of instability insert itself as a buff-
er. Their overwhelming concern is with refugee flows, so what do
we do about that?

Mr. SHERMAN. And we would hope that a prosperous unified Korean would be able to accommodate the resettlement of all residents of North and South Korea in a newly prosperous state, but I'm going to go on to another issue, and that is that we're told exports are good, but imports don't matter; that where the statistics indicate that exports will grow, we embrace the statistics; where the statistics indicate that imports will grow, well, we dismiss the statistics because there's always something fuzzy about a statistic. We're told that if we export 50,000 cars, that produces jobs. If we import 500,000 cars, well, that has no affect on our economy.

Our school systems should be able to teach subtraction as well as addition. Every other country in the world knows that it's about trade balances, that if you increase exports by 1 billion but you increase imports by 2 billion, you devastate your economy. And the only country that doesn't understand that is the country that is experiencing the largest trade deficit in the history of mammalian life.

We can hold up an iPhone as a symbol of trade, but the real symbol are the broken families in every district in this country where jobs have been lost, families have been broken up.

Now, we're told—we were told before MFN for China that the effect would be negligible on trade flows. That was off by $3 trillion. We were told that the deal with Korea would benefit us as far as our trade deficit and, in fact, we have had a spectacular increase in our trade deficit with South Korea. And now there apparently aren't even any economic studies, they're not even promising to help the U.S. economy.

Mr. Mulloy, are there—what do the economic studies which have consistently understated the devastation of these agreements, what do these economic studies show about this agreement?

Mr. MULLOY. I've been reading a lot about TPP.

Mr. SHERMAN. Your microphone.

Mr. MULLOY. Yes, I've been reading a lot about the TPP. What I see always in any spokesperson in favor of the TPP, they talk about increased American exports. I have not seen any studies, or what is going to be the impact on our trade balance with those TPP countries. Is it going to improve?

We're running a pretty major deficit with those countries right now. Will the TPP improve that? I have not seen any study that supports that.

Mr. SHERMAN. The proponents of this can't even figure out a way to lie to us. That's exceptional, so there aren't—the last few times they've been able to tell us that they're going to increase net jobs in the United States, and now they've retreated. You and I would specify yes, these agreements will create increased exports to some degree.

Mr. MULLOY. If I could speak to just one more thing.

Mr. SHERMAN. Yes.

Mr. MULLOY. Under the Constitution, you guys have control over trade.

Mr. SHERMAN. Tell that to the administration, but go on.

Mr. MULLOY. And my understanding is the majority of both Houses of Congress have written to the administration asking them to address exchange rates in the TPP.

Mr. SHERMAN. Well, let me—because I've got a response from the administration, if the chairman will indulge me. Every time I talk about them cheating on their currency, China particularly, the response is, ''But they're cheating less.'' Gentlemen, don't try that on your wives. Honey, I'm cheating less.

The idea that we would violate every day as the Executive Branch does the law compelling them to designate China as a trade—as a currency manipulator on the theory that they're treating—that they're cheating less demonstrates that no future trade agreement is going to be enforced no matter what the provisions might be. We'll scurry around, we'll file papers, but we won't do anything serious. I believe my time has expired.

Mr. SALMON. Thank you. Mr. Goodman, I'm going to give you a chance. We're going to go through one more round. We have three folks, and we'll go through another round of questions. But, Mr. Goodman, I'd like to give you a chance to respond to some of the issues that were raised.

Mr. GOODMAN. Thank you, Mr. Chairman. I'd just like to make three quick points.

First, there are studies that show the potential benefit of TPP. The Peterson Institute did a study a year or two ago that showed that the annual income gains from a completed TPP agreement in 2025 would be roughly 225 billion U.S. dollars. That's a global number. And for the United States, $76.6 billion. That's based on an econometric analysis that covers both exports and imports. I'm happy to put that specific reference in front of you. I think I may have referred to it in my written testimony, but happy to get that citation to you. So, there are studies showing potential benefits.

Of course, these numbers are not going to be absolute. The $.6 billion I take with a grain of salt, but I do think there are studies showing there's some significant income gains for the United States that come both from the export, and as I was trying to suggest earlier, the import side of the equation. So, that leads to my second point.

Globalization is a reality. Globalization and technological change are realities regardless of trade agreements. They're happening, and so the question in my mind is whether we are going to be able to positioned, and when I say we, I mean broadly the United States, including middle class workers, are going to be able to be competitive in that globalized technologically advanced, and changing world. And, to me, trade agreements run the possibility of establishing a set of rules which would level the playing field, and give us a chance to compete. So, that's what they're about.

I don't think they are going to make globalization or—the existence of them or nonexistence of them is not going to make globalization or change.

Mr. SHERMAN. If I can interrupt for a second.

Mr. GOODMAN. And I'm happy to——

Mr. SHERMAN. If I can interrupt for a second. The idea that the greatest companies in the world, the greatest workers in this world are losing by $300 billion or $400 billion a year in terms of our trade deficit, because they're bad workers, and we have fair trade is one view. The other view is that we have the greatest workers, and we have the worst rules. But it's clear we're losing, and I don't think we should blame our workers for that. I think we should blame our Government for that.

Mr. GOODMAN. Totally agree. I think that it's not our workers. Our workers are the best in the world, and our economy is the strongest in the world. We can compete if there's a level playing field, which there is not. And that's why trying to shape the rules is what these trade agreements are trying to do. Of course, they're not going to solve every problem, but I think that's what they're aspiring to do.

Just on currency really quickly, I would say that there is a currency problem in East Asia, a currency manipulation problem. Most countries in East Asia have engaged in that practice at some point or the other, and it has been a persistent problem and challenge.

My own view is that using a trade agreement to solve that problem is unlikely to be successful, and that there should be other mechanisms explored to try to promote fairness in currency practices.

Mr. SALMON. I'd like to move to a different issue. Several of you have mentioned that it's critical that the U.S. be seen by our allies in the region as a stable, consistent ally. Do you believe that's the view of the U.S. today in the region? Let me start with you, Dr. Jackson.

Mr. VAN JACKSON. So, if you had asked me 2 years ago, there would have been much greater doubts. There are still hesitations, there are still concerns, not least because it's kind of a bottomless well with some of our allies. But they feel much more confident about the U.S. today and the trajectory we're on than 2 years ago, but it's not constant. So, like if you're checking in right now, I would say that we're in a better place than we were, but there's always room for improvement.

Mr. SALMON. Mr. Denmark, do you have any thoughts on that?

Mr. DENMARK. Sure. Our allies and our partners in the Asia-Pacific are in a very difficult geopolitical position in that there's a major strategic rival or challenge very close to them, and their primary ally guarantor of their security is far away, so they're very sensitive to indications that the United States be consistent, be reliable. So, the challenge that we have as being the dominant power is that if we demonstrate our reliability and consistency 90 times, and twice we stumble, all we're going to hear about is the two times that we've stumbled. So, I've been hosting groups of people from our ally countries when we had government shutdown, and those sorts of events that we have when the government shuts down for reasons that are very difficult to explain to them, raises their concerns about how reliable we are, how we can act as a responsible country.

Further, being able to pass TPP after we have encouraged them to do it, after we've been negotiating for so long, if we're not able to pass it, that would send a signal to our allies that we're not a reliable partner, that we're not able to follow through with what we say we're going to do. So, they're very sensitive to that. They want to be able to work with us. They see themselves as needing us economically, politically, militarily, strategically, but they need to make sure that we're consistent and reliable.

82

Mr. SALMON. Dr. Karl Jackson.

Mr. KARL JACKSON. Yes, I guess I would have a twofold view on this. First of all, in the last 40 years of going back and forth, especially to Southeast Asia, I've almost never heard anyone say gee whiz, you guys are doing a terrific job. Now, we can't have been wrong consistently all the time so there is a tendency to try to poke us a little bit to get us to do a little bit more. That's one side of my answer, that is that this is a perennial complaint about us.

The other side of the answer is that if, after having said that we will rebalance to Asia, we fall down on those commitments and under-resource the rebalance to Asia, then they will begin to really doubt whether or not we are at all reliable. Thank you.

Mr. SALMON. Well, do you feel that right now our policies in our Government are adequately resourcing that pivot?

Mr. KARL JACKSON. I think the pivot is under-resourced to the extent that the change is occurring slowly. The folks in Southeast Asia tend not to notice the changes, and they tend to pocket whatever the changes are and say but, what have you done for me lately? So, it's a very careful balance, and if the Defense budget, particularly as it has an impact on U.S. presence in Asia, and particularly U.S. presence in the South China Sea were to go down, or if it wasn't responsive to increased activities on the part of the Chinese Navy, then doubts would increase. And those increases in doubt would be based upon empirical fact rather than upon just a desire to get the Americans more involved.

Mr. SALMON. I just have one last question, and then I'll yield to the ranking member. We've seen a lot of very erratic and irresponsible behavior out of North Korea, and that's probably the understatement of the century. But as far as threat level to the United States, how serious is the threat of Kim Jong-un?

Mr. VAN JACKSON. So, I wouldn't put too much credence on threats that they're going to attack the White House, or the Continental United States, or even Hawaii today. In 5 or 10 years, it's a completely different—my answer could be completely different. But when they make threats—so, their threat level is always at the, you know, intolerable level, and most of the time it's incredible, but most of the time when they engage in sort of low-level violence, or the novel forms like the Sony hack, they do signal ahead of time that they're going to do this. They do threaten that they're going to do things like this. Like the Sony hack played out over a series of months, and then the question is, you know, how do you separate signal from noise? And that's always the challenge with North Korea. But I would say that there is an upper limit, and so it's reasonable to not take as seriously. Well, I mean, if you're in the military you should take it all seriously, but you don't need to take as seriously some of the bombast about, you know, global annihilation. But the stuff—if they're saying they're going to hack a South Korean bank, or if they say they're going to go after a corporate actor in the U.S., I would take that extremely seriously, because they've shown that that's—they're willing to match word and deed on those smaller scale acts.

Mr. SALMON. Thank you. I yield to the gentleman.

Mr. SHERMAN. Mr. Jackson brings up this hacking of Sony which, of course, was designed to chill free speech in America. I'd point out China has bought AMC, or a Chinese businessman working with the Chinese Government, and so I wonder whether we'll see any more movies made about Tibet, or a movie made about Tiananmen knowing that so many of the screens around the country may not air it; this at the same time while the Chinese Government, while claiming to be part of WTO, doesn't allow our movies free access to their screens.

Mr. Denmark, I have to disagree with you on something that you probably don't even realize you said. You said, "Asians will think we can't get it passed." We, means the Executive Branch in that sentence. That is a misunderstanding of the United States Constitution. We are the American people. We under Article I of the Constitution are the United States Congress. We in Congress are given the authority to deal with international commerce, and the only thing we have agreed on is that this currency manipulation has to stop. We—to say that the American President can go out there, make promises, and then say Congress is unpatriotic or letting America down, or besmirching America's word because we don't do what he says, is a device used to dismantle our Constitution, and has been done by many administrations.

Again, Mr. Jackson, we're now deploying, Mr. Mulloy says, 60 percent of our Air Force, 60 percent of our Naval power to the Pacific mostly to fight over some rocks that Japan claims, as much as anything else. How much does Japan spend as a percentage of its GDP on its defense? Isn't it below 1 percent?

Mr. KARL JACKSON. It's characteristically below 1 percent. Their defense budget, however, has been going up for the last 3 years.

Mr. SHERMAN. And it still remains under 1 percent?

Mr. KARL JACKSON. Yes. It once exceeded 1 percent, and I was there that afternoon and helped make it happen.

Mr. SHERMAN. Congratulations. So, we spend 4 or 5 percent of our GDP, more if you throw in veterans benefits, which after all is part of our military pay structure. And, as I pointed out, there isn't any oil under those islands, but if there was, we don't get any of it.

I want to go to this idea that this trade deal benefits us. Mr. Mulloy, in general, to the extent there have been benefits from trade, they've gone to Wall Street, and the harm of trade has hit American working families. Is there any study out there that shows that there are more jobs in the United States net after imports from TPP, as currently configured?

Mr. MULLOY. First, the study that Mr. Goodman cited by the Petersen Institute, I know the administration used that. And then Glenn Kessler in The Washington Post investigated that claim and gave it four Pinnochios. It might be worthwhile to get that article from The Washington Post and put it in the record of the hearing.

Mr. SHERMAN. Without objection we'll do that. Go on.

Mr. MULLOY. Now, I think when the TPP is concluded, it's not concluded yet, I think under the law, the ITC is supposed to give an economic analysis looking at its total impact on the American economy, which I think will have to get into the whole business of a trade balance and jobs.

There is a formula that economists use for determining GDP. They use investment, consumption, government spending, and then

84

net exports. When net exports are negative, they are detracting from GDP and job growth, and that means that your economy is not performing the way it would if you weren't running the negative net exports. You'd probably grow your economy 2 or 3 percent more than it would happen if you run the major deficit in net exports. That would result in better paying jobs for Americans, and I think better communities.

And I think the way we've run it now, the corporations are focused on shareholder value. Other countries put in place policies that make it good for them to outsource. For example, if you produce in China and then ship back, that underpriced currency gives you an export subsidy and helps you make greater profits. It also makes it more difficult for you to sell from here into China.

Mr. SHERMAN. If I can interrupt, one good example is the Chinese realize they're going to import planes from the United States, so they require Boeing to make the fuselages in China, and then those fuselages are shipped and used all over the world. And they're able to do that while being in WTO because the government controls the decision as to whether they're going to buy Airbus, or they're going to buy Boeing.

Here, our airlines will buy a Brazilian plane or a Canadian plane based on what's in the interest of the airline; whereas, the Chinese airlines are doing what's—based on what's in the interest of China as defined by its government. And with those kinds of rules, we're going to lose airplane manufacturing one airplane part at a time.

Mr. MULLOY. One of my recommendations in my written statement is that we ought to give an antitrust protection, where if Boeing wanted to go to Airbus and say let's both of us agree that we're not going to be transferring technology as part of making a sale to China; that we should give them the right to do that, so that they're not squeezed by the Chinese. The Chinese will say to Boeing if you don't do this, then we'll buy from Airbus. Well, the two of them ought to get together. And I think the Europeans might be interested in some kind of a relationship like that, because this is going on across the board.

Our companies are told that if you invest more and move R&D into China, you'll be considered friends of China. But what's happening is, those transfers of technology and R&D are beefing up the Chinese ability to build their defense industrial base, and their military base. So, I think we need to really focus on this whole China relationship and get that as a key part of the rebalancing to Asia. And it will strengthen our whole geopolitical position if we get this relationship more balanced.

Mr. SHERMAN. Thank you.

Mr. SALMON. Well, thank you. It looks like the questions are through. I appreciate the distinguished panel coming and addressing many of our concerns. As you can see, this was the tip of the iceberg. We've got a lot to cover over the next couple of years, and we didn't even get to a lot of the questions and the concerns that the committee will have.

I appreciate everybody's participation, and this committee is now adjourned.

[Whereupon, at 11:58 a.m., the subcommittee was adjourned.]

APPENDIX

MATERIAL SUBMITTED FOR THE RECORD

86

SUBCOMMITTEE HEARING NOTICE
COMMITTEE ON FOREIGN AFFAIRS
U.S. HOUSE OF REPRESENTATIVES
WASHINGTON, DC 20515-6128

Subcommittee on Asia and the Pacific
Matt Salmon (R-AZ), Chairman

February 25, 2015

TO: MEMBERS OF THE COMMITTEE ON FOREIGN AFFAIRS

You are respectfully requested to attend an OPEN hearing of the Committee on Foreign Affairs, to be held by the Subcommittee on Asia and the Pacific in Room 2172 of the Rayburn House Office Building (and available live on the Committee website at http://www.ForeignAffairs.house.gov):

DATE: Thursday, February 26, 2015

TIME: 10:00 a.m.

SUBJECT: Across the Other Pond: U.S. Opportunities and Challenges in the Asia Pacific

WITNESSES: Karl D. Jackson, Ph.D.
                 C.V. Starr Distinguished Professor of Southeast Asia Studies
                 Director of the Asian Studies Program
                 Johns Hopkins School of Advanced International Studies

                 Van Jackson, Ph.D.
                 Visiting Fellow
                 Center for a New American Security

                 Mr. Matthew P. Goodman
                 William E. Simon Chair in Political Economy
                 Senior Adviser for Asian Economics
                 Center for Strategic and International Studies

                 Mr. Abraham M. Denmark
                 Senior Vice President
                 Political and Security Affairs and External Relations
                 The National Bureau of Asian Research

                 The Honorable Patrick Mulloy
                 Trade Lawyer
                 (*Former Commissioner, U.S.-China Economic and Security Commission*)

By Direction of the Chairman

COMMITTEE ON FOREIGN AFFAIRS

MINUTES OF SUBCOMMITTEE ON _____ *Asia and the Pacific* _____ HEARING

Day___*Thursday*___Date___*February 26*___Room_____*2172*_____

Starting Time ____*10:04*____ Ending Time ___*11:59*___

Recesses _____ (____to____) (____to____) (____to____) (____to____) (____to____) (____to____)

Presiding Member(s)

Matt Salmon

Check all of the following that apply:

Open Session ☑   Electronically Recorded (taped) ☑
Executive (closed) Session ☐   Stenographic Record ☐
Televised ☐

TITLE OF HEARING:

Across the Other Pond: U.S. Opportunities and Challenges in the Asia Pacific

SUBCOMMITTEE MEMBERS PRESENT:

Dana Rohrabacher, Steve Chabot, Brad Sherman, Ami Bera, Alan Lowenthal, Gerald Connolly, Grace Meng

NON-SUBCOMMITTEE MEMBERS PRESENT: *(Mark with an * if they are not members of full committee.)*

HEARING WITNESSES: Same as meeting notice attached? Yes ☑ No ☐
(If "no", please list below and include title, agency, department, or organization.)

STATEMENTS FOR THE RECORD: *(List any statements submitted for the record.)*

Gerald Connolly

TIME SCHEDULED TO RECONVENE _____
or
TIME ADJOURNED ____*11:58*____

_____
Subcommittee Staff Director

Statement for the Record
Submitted by Mr. Connolly of Virginia

The strategic rebalance to the Asia-Pacific region is not an expedition into parts unknown. As we further define this policy shift, now in its fourth year, we should seek guidance from models in the region that embody the principles of the rebalance; supporting economic integration and trade, enhancing regional security, advancing inclusive economic development, strengthening regional institutions, and addressing health and environmental issues. As the U.S. makes decisions on where to expend limited resources, adapting best practices where we have successfully promoted democracy or developed a close alliance could avoid a costly trial and error approach. This strategy would also underline the longstanding commitments the U.S. has maintained in the Asia-Pacific.

Of the 11 nations with which the U.S. is currently negotiating the Trans-Pacific Partnership (TPP), 6 already have free trade agreements (FTAs) with the U.S. A primary objective of the rebalance is to support economic integration and trade. The TPP negotiations represent an opportunity to expand on robust economic ties our nation has to the region. The participating nations comprise 40 percent of the global economy and account for nearly one-third of global trade. A high-quality TPP agreement would lower barriers to trade with Japan, currently our 4th largest trading partner, create new opportunities for American businesses in Malaysia, one of only 13 countries in the world to record an average growth of 7 percent per year for 25 years or more, and allow us to potentially expand the participants at a later date to regional partners like Korea and Taiwan. Through deepened economic ties with the region, the U.S. will be well-positioned to shape trade and industry practices, and the U.S should use the negotiations to insist on strong labor and environmental protections, particularly in countries where we have concerns about current standards. We cannot be satisfied with just any deal. The deal must be consistent with our values and advance our interests in the region.

The U.S. already maintains an enduring commitment to the people of the Asia-Pacific. For decades, we have deployed American diplomacy and development assistance to promote democracy, human rights, global health, and economic prosperity. This has come in the form of life-saving food assistance, protection against infectious diseases, support for national reconciliation efforts, and regional programs such as the Lower Mekong Initiative. Where we have planted seeds of civil society or bolstered democratic gains, we should hope to build on that success through the rebalance.

We have relationships in the region where this approach has paid dividends. At the beginning of the U.S.-Korea alliance, Korea was an impoverished country. It has since experienced dramatic economic and democratic gains. Korea is now a democracy of 51 million people. It has the 12th largest economy in the world and the 29th largest GDP per capita ($35K). It is a strategically valuable relationship important to addressing threats on the Korean peninsula, constraining North

Korea, and ultimately reunifying the peninsula under a democratic government. A longtime recipient of foreign aid, Korea became a donor of official development assistance in 1987. In 2010, Korea became the first country to have ever moved from being a recipient of international development assistance to a donor and a member of the Development Assistance Committee (DAC) of the Organization for Economic Co-operation and Development (OECD). Korea is also wrapping up a very active two-year stint on the United Nations Security Council. Twenty-five years ago, Korea was not even a full member of the United Nations. The U.S.-Korea alliance is a strong one that was forged in blood. It has since grown according to the model we should hope to emulate for our relationships in the Asia-Pacific.

Deepening our relationships in the Asia-Pacific will not be without its challenges. China is already wary of a heightened U.S. presence in the region. However, China cannot be allowed to dictate the trajectory of our engagement. China's assertive posture towards maritime disputes in the South and East China seas continues to be a source of division in the region and should be discouraged at every turn. We also must uphold the commitments we have made such as those enshrined in the Taiwan Relations Act. Accordingly, we should be concerned by China's aggression in the Taiwan Strait through the unilateral imposition of an Air Defense Identification Zone. The rebalance should not sacrifice our standing obligations. Instead, those steadfast commitments should be held up as a value proposition to countries seeking closer relationship with the U.S.

Regardless of the connotation of the term *rebalance*, the U.S. has a track record in the Asia-Pacific and we should use it to our benefit.